MASTERMINDS Riddle Math *Series*

DECIMALS, PERCENTAGES, METRIC SYSTEM, AND CONSUMER MATH

Reproducible Skill Builders And Higher Order Thinking Activities Based On NCTM Standards

By Brenda Opie, Lory Jackson, and Douglas McAvinn

Incentive Publications, Inc.
Nashville, Tennessee

Illustrated by Douglas McAvinn
Cover illustration by Douglas McAvinn

ISBN 0-86530-301-0

PRINTED IN THE UNITED STATES OF AMERICA

TABLE OF CONTENTS

BRAIN CHALLENGERS: DECIMALS, PERCENTAGES
METRIC SYSTEM, AND CONSUMER MATH

NAME_____

THE INFAMOUS DECIMAL POINT!

DIRECTIONS: Make a list of 10 to 16 different ways decimals can be used in your daily life. Use the example of money only once.

1. _____
2. _____
3. _____
4. _____
5. _____
6. _____
7. _____
8. _____

9. _____
10. _____
11. _____
12. _____
13. _____
14. _____
15. _____
16. _____

DIRECTIONS: List 5 to 6 ways our lives might be different if decimals were suddenly removed from our number system.

1. _____
2. _____
3. _____
4. _____
5. _____
6. _____

NAME_____

What did Dracula take for his cold?

DIRECTIONS: To find the solution to this question, follow these directions. First work the problems below, and then find the answer in the answer column. The number in front of the answer tells you where to put the letter of the problem in the row of boxes at the bottom of the page.

F = 6.002

N = 0.55

R = 8.03

S = 8.003

I = 6.2

F = 8.3

D = 0.5

P = 6.02

O = 0.038

C = 0.38

O = 0.055

1. thirty-eight hundredths

2. thirty-eight thousandths

3. eight and three tenths

4. six and two thousandths

5. six and two tenths

6. fifty-five hundredths

7. five tenths

8. eight and three hundredths

9. fifty-five thousandths

10. six and two hundredths

11. eight and three thousandths

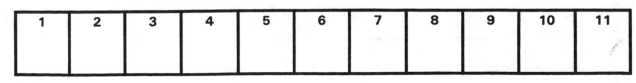

1	2	3	4	5	6	7	8	9	10	11

NAME _____

Why did the covered wagon break down on the prairie?

DIRECTIONS: Write each decimal word name as a standard decimal numeral. Each time your answer appears in the secret code, write the letter of the problem above it.

1. Seven hundred thirty-three and two hundredths _____ (T)

2. Forty-three thousandths _____ (B)

3. Twelve and three hundred forty-two thousandths _____ (H)

4. One thousand, three hundred eight and nine tenths _____ (U)

5. Eight and five hundredths _____ (E)

6. Ninety-seven and three thousandths _____ (D)

7. Eight and five thousandths _____ (R)

8. Two and four tenths _____ (W)

9. Thirteen and five hundredths _____ (L)

10. Six and seven thousandths _____ (O)

11. Forty-three hundredths _____ (A)

12. Nine tenths _____ (I)

_____ _____ _____ _____ _____ _____ _____
.9   733.02   97.003

_____ _____ _____ _____ _____ _____
12.342 .43   8.05

_____ _____ _____ _____ _____ _____ _____
2.4   12.342   13.05   8.05   733.02   8.005   13.05   6.007   1308.9   .043   13.05   8.05

Using graphs to read decimal notation

What did the buffalo say to his son when he went away on a long trip?

DIRECTIONS: Count the number of hundredths that are shaded in each of the graphs below, and write your answer in decimal notation in the appropriate space below the graph. Locate your answer in the decoder. Each time it occurs, write the letter of the problem above it.

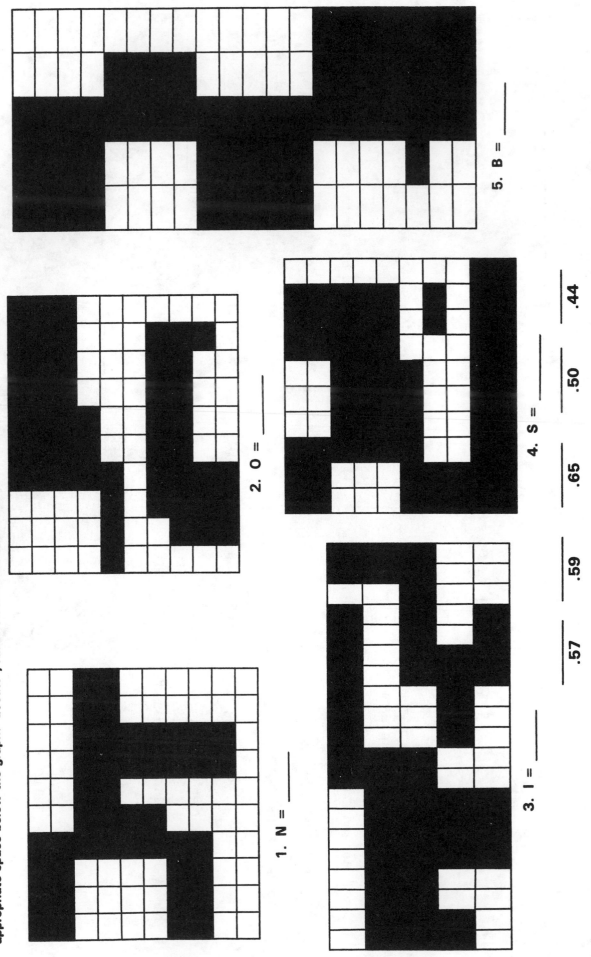

1. N = _____

2. O = _____

3. I = _____

4. S = _____

5. B = _____

_____   _____   _____   _____   _____   _____
.57   .59   .65   .50   .44

Decimal Design

DIRECTIONS: The design below contains one hundred parts because one whole in decimal notation contains one hundred parts. Count the number of hundredths that exist in each part of the design and fill in the appropriate space at the bottom of the page in decimal notation. When you finish, add all of these parts together. You will know you are correct if all parts total one whole or 1.00.

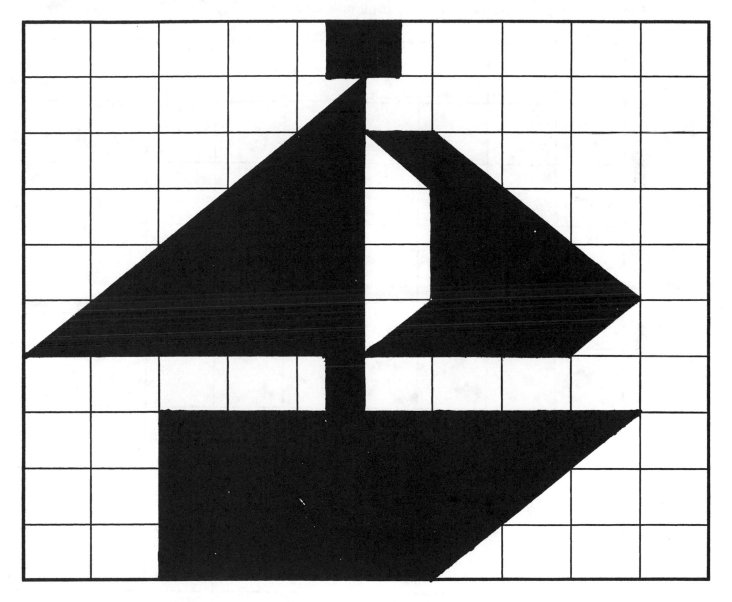

Hull (body of boat) = _____

Mast (support for the sails) = _____

Crow's Nest (lookout) = _____

Large sail = _____

Small sail = _____

Background = _____

Using higher order thinking skills to create a decimal design

NAME_____

Create your own decimal design

DIRECTIONS: Create a design that will in some way use all of the hundredths in the graph given below. When you finish, make a key with the different components of your graph listed. Give your graph to a friend, and let him/her fill in the key. To know if the key has been done correctly, all the parts should total one whole or 1.00.

NAME_____

Decimal Skill Test - Decimal Notation

DIRECTIONS: Write the decimal in the space provided by each problem.

1. 4 and 3 tenths = _____

2. 9 and 26 thousandths = _____

3. 52 thousandths = _____

4. 7 and 3 hundredths = _____

5. 296 thousandths = _____

6. 8 and 9 ten thousandths = _____

7. 7 and 4 hundred thousandths = _____

8. 643 and 7 tenths = _____

9. 3 and 2 thousandths = _____

10. 8 and 6 hundredths = _____

DIRECTIONS: Write the word name for the decimal notations given below.

1. .33 = _____

2. 7.04 = _____

3. .670 = _____

4. 72. 0004 = _____

_____

5. 3.1 = _____

6. .84 = _____

7. 8.004 = _____

_____

8. .007 = _____

9. 600.43 = _____

_____

10. 7,435 .01 = _____

_____

SCORE _____

SCORE _____

Writing decimal notations (tenths to hundred thousandths)

NAME_____

CROSS-NUMBER PUZZLE

DIRECTIONS: Each dot is a decimal point in the cross-number puzzle. Write the standard numerals in the blanks provided. Then, put the decimal notations in the puzzle so they will all fit. Numbers may run either across or down. Two problems have been done for you.

7	3	4	9	8		
	.					
		.				
			.			
				.		
					.	
	3	3	7	3	0	

1. Thirty-three thousand, seven hundred thirty   <u>33,730</u>

2. Seventy-three thousand four hundred ninety-eight   <u>73,498</u>

3. Seven hundred sixty-eight thousand, nine hundred twenty-six _____

4. Nine hundred twenty-four thousand, three hundred ninety _____

5. Three and ninety ten thousandths _____

6. Six and fourteen thousand thirty-nine hundred thousandths _____

7. Two thousand nine hundred eighty-seven and forty-three hundredths_____

8. Nine hundred forty and seven hundred thirty-three thousandths _____

9. Three thousand four hundred thirty-four and three tenths _____

10. Sixty thousand four hundred thirty-eight and nine tenths _____

11. Forty-one and eight hundred forty-three ten thousandths _____

12. Nine hundred and two hundred thirty-four thousandths _____

13. Eight thousand two and eighty seven hundredths _____

14. Eighty and forty-two ten thousandths _____

Determining place value in decimals

If a millionaire sits on gold, who sits on silver?

NAME

DIRECTIONS: Figure out which digit has the given place value in each of the decimals below. You will then need to write these digits, in order, into the first row of boxes at the bottom of the page. Then use the decoder key to find the numeral to put in the bottom row of boxes. You will need to fill in the bottom row from left to right.

1. 34.6786 (ten thousandths) = _____

2. 61.0297 (hundredths) = _____

3. .893 (thousandths) = _____

4. 889.02234 (hundreds) = _____

5. 159, 675.4 (ten thousands) = _____

6. 34, 567. 12 (tenths) = _____

7. 302, 451, 003, 004 (hundred billions) = _____

8. 3, 423. 8999 (ten thousandths) = _____

9. 456.8792 (hundredths) = _____

10. 315, 678, 923.1 (ten millions) = _____

11. 456. 749 (hundredths) = _____

12. 3.6098 (ones) = _____

13. 981. 3097 (thousandths) = _____

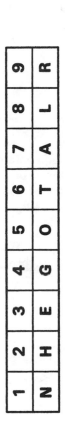

1	2	3	4	5	6	7	8	9
N	H	E	G	O	T	A	L	R

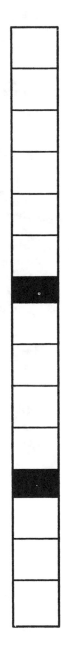

INSTRUCTIONS FOR DECIMAL BINGO

This game is played in the same manner as BINGO. The students need a board such as the one on the accompanying page. You, as the teacher, will need one master list of all the possibilities that the students may have on their boards (Example 1). Several rounds of Decimal Bingo can be played with one board. For this to occur, each game will need a different way to mark the boxes called. For example, a √, x, ☐, 0, z, ♦, etc. can be used for different rounds (Example 1). Some possibilities for games are: (1) regular Decimal Bingo which can be won by four in a row either horizontally, vertically, diagonally (Example 2); (2) four corners (Example 2); (3) postage stamp (Example 2); picture frame (Example 3); and a big "X" (Example 3). When a student has achieved marking the squares that needed to be called in order to win, he yells DECIMAL-O. The student then brings his paper to you so it can be checked for accuracy. As a perequisite for winning, the student can also be asked to read the numbers correctly. Winners can be awarded prizes such as a new pencil, eraser, computer pass, media center pass, piece of candy, etc.

Decimal Bingo can be used to practice math skills such as whole number facts, fractional equivalents, metric notation, and mathematical vocabulary. Once you use Decimal Bingo, you will discover many other areas of the curriculum in which it can be used!

◆◆◆◆◆◆◆◆◆◆◆◆◆◆◆◆

EXAMPLE 1
Teacher's Master List

1.	3.04	√ x 0 ♦
2.	.304	☐ √ ♦
3.	3.403	0 x
4.	.4	☐ √
5.	.34	x z
6.	7.896	0 z ♦
7.	.7896	√ ♦
8.	7.89	☐ √
9.	.78	0 z √
10.	7.11	0 x ♦
11.	8.9436	x ♦
12.	.8943	0 z ♦
13.	8.906	☐ √ x
14.	8.894	0 z ♦
15.	8.94	√ ♦
16.	54.32	0 x √
17.	.543	☐ x z
18.	.5	0 z ♦
19.	5.432	x z √
20.	5.5432	☐ √ ♦
21.	500.543	0 x z
22.	504.3	x z ♦
23.	6.638	☐ √

STUDENT 1 - EXAMPLE 2

STUDENT 2 - EXAMPLE 3   Big X or Picture Frame ☐

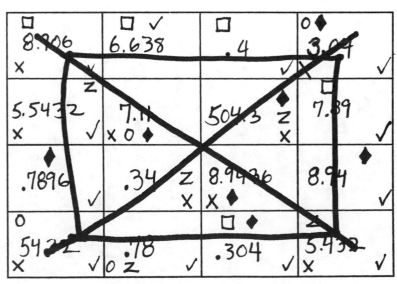

Playing Decimal Bingo to read numbers with decimals

NAME_____

DECIMAL BINGO

DIRECTIONS: Choose <u>any</u> 16 of the numbers listed below, and write them in the boxes. You are now ready to play Decimal Bingo.

1.	3.04	11.	8.9436	21.	500.543
2.	.304	12.	.8943	22.	504.3
3.	3.403	13.	8.906	23.	6.638
4.	.4	14.	8.894	24.	66.38
5.	.34	15.	8.94	25.	.663
6.	7.896	16.	54.32	26.	600.66
7.	.7896	17.	.543	27.	.6638
8.	7.89	18.	.5	28.	.6
9.	.78	19.	5.432	29.	606.638
10.	7.11	20.	5.5432	30.	.66

Comparing decimals

NAME _____

Why are spiders good baseball players?

DIRECTIONS: Choose the greatest number and circle it. Then write the letter underneath your choice in the decoder below.

#	Choice 1		Choice 2	
1.	7.8	(T)	6.34	(R)
2.	4.3	(F)	4.03	(S)
3.	6.43	(E)	7.1	(K)
4.	50.2	(H)	50.19	(V)
5.	.99	(H)	1.00	(T)
6.	2.04	(H)	1.99	(T)
7.	84.37	(P)	84.4	(W)
8.	10.09	(W)	10.1	(E)
9.	.3		.04	
10.	6.005	(Z)	9.1	(C)
11.	.999	(A)	1.9	(H)
12.	3.24	(W)	3.024	(S)
13.	.02	(L)	.005	(W)
14.	.703	(Q)	1.1	(E)
15.	1.99	(D)	99.1	(O)
16.	3.011		3.1	(I)
17.	2.75	(M)	.398	
18.	.5	(O)	1.5	(H)
19.	14.029	(N)	14.37	(Y)
20.	.009	(J)	.005	(L)
21.	2.01	(T)	.999	(V)
22.	1.8	(E)	.9	(U)
23.	.05	(F)	.2	(S)

Decoder boxes:

1.00	1.9	1.8	14.37

.3	1.1

2.01	9.1

7.1	1.5	.9	84.4

2.75	9.1

50.2	99.1	3.24

.02	3.1	10.1

4.3

.2

7.8	2.04

2.04

NAME_____

Decimal Comparisons

BACKGROUND INFORMATION: Relation symbols are used to compare two numbers. They are:

= equal
> greater than
< less than

Examples are:

24.56 > 24.32
7.09 < 7.16
57.64 = 57.640

DIRECTIONS: Compare the following decimals by using the relation symbols: =, <, or >.

1.	5.2 5.18	11.	5.25 5.2
2.	93.25 92.25	12.	97.2 96.234
3.	107.58 107.580	13.	15.03 15.003
4.	175.5 7.55	14.	59.26 592.6
5.	0.003 0.030	15.	200.02 200.002
6.	4.38 4.48	16.	3.204 3.210
7.	50.03 50.13	17.	705.37 704.37
8.	75.3 75.29	18.	145.8 156.7
9.	19.23 192.3	19.	5.049 5.14
10.	9258.3 9158.88	20.	25.130 25.13

NAME_____

Decimal Skill Test - Comparing decimals

DIRECTIONS: Write <, >, or = to compare the numbers.

1. 16.3 _____ 1.95

2. 3.17 _____ 3.170

3. 18.98 _____ 59.87

4. 58.7 _____ 59.87

5. 8.07 _____ 59.87

6. 2.6 _____ 2.599

7. 17.02 _____ 17.20

8. 0.389 _____ 0.299

9. 0.87 _____ .871

10. 30.009 _____ 30.1

11. 63.9 _____ 63.900

12. .008 _____ .1

13. 467.2 _____ 46.99

14. .01 _____ .010

15. 35.892 _____ 34.936

16. 6.22 _____ 6.33

17. 15.07 _____ 1.507

18. 64.3 _____ 64.03

19. 40.792 _____ 40.7920

20. .042 _____ .099

SCORE _____

Rounding to the nearest whole number

NAME_____

CROSS-NUMBER PUZZLE NO. 2

DIRECTIONS: Complete the puzzle.

ACROSS: Round to the nearest whole number.

A. 448.09 = _____	J. 84.9 = _____	Q. 19.04 = _____
B. 634.52 = _____	L. 12.34 = _____	R. 35.781 = _____
C. 96.7 = _____	M. 39.5 = _____	S. 403.009 = _____
F. 984.081 = _____	N. 398.9 = _____	T. 698.453 = _____
G. 13.456 = _____	O. 485.675 = _____	U. 43.985 = _____
I. 34.7 = _____	P. 843.56 = _____	

DOWN: Round to the nearest whole number.

A. 4691.7 = _____	I. 396.02 = _____	O. 449.06 = _____
D. 437.3 = _____	J. 810.009 = _____	P. 812.9 = _____
E. 85.1 = _____	K. 352.410 = _____	R. 308.2 = _____
F. 9159.06 = _____	M. 463.09 = _____	S. 49.009 = _____
H. 83.009 = _____	N. 384.074 = _____	V. 604.3 = _____

Rounding decimals to the nearest tenth

NAME_____

TICKLE YOUR FUNNY BONE

DIRECTIONS: Round each number to the nearest tenth. Find your answer in the secret code. Each time your answer appears in the secret code, write the letter of the problem above it.

1. 718.43 = _____ (N)
2. 474.065 = _____ (U)
3. 7,438.43 = _____ (Y)
4. 69.084 = _____ (L)
5. 3.567 = _____ (D)
6. 43.94 = _____ (C)
7. 38.05 = _____ (K)
8. 100.501 = _____ (A)
9. 2.840 = _____ (O)

10. 2,634.55 = _____ (B)
11. 0.56 = _____ (M)
12. 49.982 = _____ (E)
13. 58.099 = _____ (I)
14. 109.96 = _____ (H)
15. 399.742 = _____ (W)
16. 9,999.99 = _____ (S)
17. 0.328 = _____ (T)

PARADISE:

__	__	__	__	__	__	__	__
.3	399.7	2.8	399.7	110.0	58.1	.3	50.0

__	__	__	__	__	__	__	__	__
43.9	474.1	2,634.6	50.0	10,000.0	399.7	58.1	.3	110.0

__	__	__	__	__	__	__	__	__
2,634.6	69.1	100.5	43.9	38.1	3.6	2.8	.3	10,000.0

CLIMATE:

__	__	__	__	__	__	__
399.7	110.0	100.5	.3	7,438.4	2.8	474.1

__	__	__	__	__
3.6	2.8	.3	2.8	100.5

__	__	__	__	__	__	__
.6	2.8	474.1	718.4	.3	100.5	58.1	718.4

What did the big hand say to the little hand?

DIRECTIONS: Solve each problem and find your answer in the decoder. Each time it occurs in the decoder, write the letter of the problem above it.

Round to the nearest tenth:

1. 678.34 = _____ (A)

2. .945 = _____ (N)

3. 678.365 = _____ (O)

4. 1.9432 = _____ (U)

5. 1.834 = _____ (G)

6. .9536 = _____ (E)

Round each number to the nearest hundredth:

7. 11.834 = _____ (Y)

8. 1.9367 = _____ (C)

9. 13.056 = _____ (L)

10. 11.867 = _____ (I)

11. 1.9578 = _____ (W)

Round to the nearest thousandth:

12. 5.3479 = _____ (K)

13. 5.3972 = _____ (R)

14. .9565 = _____ (H)

15. 5.9874 = _____ (D)

16. .9753 = _____ (B)

17. 1.2456 = _____ (T)

5.987	678.4	.9	1.246	1.8	678.4	678.3	1.96	678.3	11.83

11.87	13.06	13.06	.975	1.0	.975	678.3	1.94	5.348

11.87	.9	678.3	.9	.957	678.4	1.9	5.397

**Rounding to the nearest whole number,
tenth, hundredth, and thousandth**

NAME_____

Decimal Skill Test- Rounding

Round to the nearest whole number.

1. 612.39 = _____

2. 348.075 = _____

3. 86.74 = _____

4. 1036.50 = _____

5. 0.9 = _____

6. 39.99 = _____

7. 889.57 = _____

8. .42 = _____

Round to the nearest tenth.

9. 347.68 = _____

10. .93 = _____

11. 426.73 = _____

12. 806.95 = _____

13. 34.989 = _____

14. 51.04 = _____

15. 386.55 = _____

16. .568 = _____

Round to the nearest hundredth.

17. 57.843 = _____

18. 609.398 = _____

19. .067 = _____

20. 0.439 = _____

21. 69.998 = _____

22. 0.993 = _____

23. 43.692 = _____

24. 0.942 = _____

Round to the nearest thousandth

25. .0094 = _____

26. 23.9804 = _____

27. .9806 = _____

28. .0982 = _____

29. 1.6782 = _____

30. 21.3561 = _____

31. 3.0976 = _____

32. 100.4788 = _____

SCORE _____

Adding decimals

NAME_____

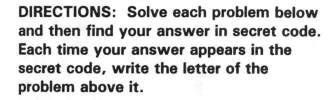

What was I?

DIRECTIONS: Solve each problem below and then find your answer in secret code. Each time your answer appears in the secret code, write the letter of the problem above it.

BACKGROUND INFORMATION: I was 13 feet from my nose to my tail, and I stood about 6 feet tall. I had a sickle-like claw on each foot which I used to tear open the stomachs of other dinosaurs during combat. My claw toe stayed off the ground when I ran to keep from being broken or dulled by the underbrush. My large, sharp teeth curved backward, giving me the ability to tear huge chunks of my prey's flesh.

1. 7.84 + 3.987 + .004 + 7 = _____(H)

2. 9 + .092 + .0008 + 6.7 = _____ (U)

3. 8.4 + .009 + 3 = _____ (O)

4. .009 + 4 = _____ (I)

5. 6.43 + 7.890 + .03 + .1 = _____ (N)

6. .74 + .009 + 8.436 = _____ (E)

7. 4456 + .09 + 1.45 + .008 = _____ (S)

8. .10 + 1.09 + 8.763 = _____ (D)

9. 3 + 4.65 + .3 = _____ (C)

10. .8 + .09 = _____ (Y)

9.953	9.185	4.009	14.45	11.409	14.45	.89	7.95	18.831	15.7928	4457.548

Adding decimals

What's Beethoven doing today?

DIRECTIONS: Solve each problem on another sheet of paper. Find your answer in the decoder, and each time your answer occurs, write the letter of the problem above it.

NAME _____

1. $756.9 + 0.79 =$ _____ (N)

2. $.037 + .04 + .625 + .7 =$ _____ (P)

3. $29 + 486.89 + 298.5 =$ _____ (C)

4. $17.6 + .62 + .009 + 9.41 =$ _____ (S)

5. $3.854 + 14.15 + 8.9083 + 4.4 =$ _____ (I)

6. $2.34 + 0.765 + 3.877 =$ _____ (E)

7. $.073 + 6.2 + 7.18 =$ _____ (G)

8. $19.41 + 7 =$ _____ (O)

9. $7.575 + 87 =$ _____ (M)

10. $0.1 + 0.8 + 7.8 =$ _____ (D)

___ ___ ___ ___ ___ ___ ___ ___ ___ ___ ___ ___ ___ ___ ___
8.7 6.982 814.39 26.41 94.575 1.402 26.41 27.639 31.3123 757.69 13.453

Subtracting decimals

NAME_____

MATH BINGO

DIRECTIONS: Work the problems on another sheet of paper, and then find your answers in the bingo box below. Circle the answer. When you have circled five answers in a line either horizontally, diagonally, or vertically, you have a Math Bingo.

20.35	2.2	$71.09	$92.20	0.642
4.615	$35.02	5.723	38.36	0.08
1.435	1.27	**FREE SPACE**	12.121	$87.56
22.3	4.56	$87.69	$4.79	47.28
6.15	0.598	2.923	0.869	94.387

1.   52.68 - 5.4 = _____

2.   3.1 - .177 = _____

3.   6.023 - 1.408 = _____

4.   74.36 - 36 = _____

5.   9.36 - 4.8 = _____

6. $77.48 - $6.39 = _____

7. $7.61 - $2.82 = _____

8.   32 - 25.85 = _____

9.   7 - 4.8 = _____

10. $92.36 - $4.80 = _____

11.   9 - 7.73 = _____

12.   2.767 - 1.898 = _____

13.   37 - 16.65 = _____

14. $230.00 - $137.80 = _____

15.   38.5 - 16.2 = _____

16.   8 - 7.402 = _____

17.   0.8 - 0.72 = _____

18.   6.435 - 0.712 = _____

19.   15.74 - 3.619 = _____

NAME _____

What do you have when 500 Indians can't buy any apples?

Subtracting decimals

DIRECTIONS: First, solve each of the problems. Second, find your answer in the decoder at the bottom of the page. Third, each time your answer appears in the decoder, write the letter or digit of the problem above it.

1. 9 - 3.625 =   (S)

2. 36 - .45 =   (H)

3. .8 - .565 =   (D)

4. 6 - 2.41 =   (A)

5. 74 - 52.8 =   (N)

6. 3.6 - 1.19 =   (5)

7. 7.4 - 6.832 =   (L)

8. 15 - 7.64 =   (E)

9. 39 - 3.65 =   (P)

10. 3 - .007 =   (I)

11. 48.5 - 37.837 =   (T)

12. 600 - .6 =   (O)

10.663	35.55	7.36		

2.993	21.2	.235	2.993	.568	35.35	7.36	3.59	5.375	5.375	2.41	599.4	599.4

3.59	35.35	.568	7.36	21.2

What happens if an ax falls on your car?

DIRECTIONS: Estimate each sum or difference, and then find your answer in the decoder. Each time your answer occurs, write the letter of the problem above it.

1.   6.88 + 1.197 = _____ (E)

2. $8.89 - $2.10 = _____ (V)

3.   15.75 + 4.18 = _____ (O)

4.   4.09 + 14.8 + 2.01 = _____ (I)

5.   11.175 - 1.97 = _____ (U)

6. $20.00 - $14.89 = _____ (D)

7.   2.1794 + 19.02 + 36.195 = _____(N)

8. $41.91 - $26.87 = _____ (Y)

9.   19.83 + 5.1 + 4.9 + 2.8 = _____(T)

10. $13.75 + $5.10 + $2.87 = _____(H)

11. $44.86 - $26.99 = _____ (X)

12. 2.194 + 19.85 + 36.003 = _____ (A)

___ ___ ___ ___ ___ ___ ___ ___ ___
$15.00   20   9 $22.00   58 $7.00   8   58   57

___ ___ ___ ___ ___ ___ ___
58   $18.00   21 $5.00   8   57   33

©1995 by Incentive Publications, Inc., Nashville, TN.

NAME _____

Where do mummies go on vacation?

DIRECTIONS: Solve each problem below on another sheet of paper. Each time your answer occurs in the decoder, write the letter of the problem above it.

1. $10 - 6.35 =$ _____ (D)

2. $.7 + 4.3 + 8 + 6.91 =$ _____ (H)

3. $.789 + 3.496 + 10 + .008 =$ _____ (O)

4. $8.974 - 3.2 =$ _____ (S)

5. $(16.923 - 4.37) + 2.8 =$ _____ (T)

6. $(8.3 + 7) - (6 - 2.3) =$ _____ (R)

7. $94.32 - 68.94 =$ _____ (I)

8. $(9 - 3.02) + (6.35 - 1.49) =$ _____ (E)

9. $74 + .06 + 7.08 + 3.71 =$ _____ (P)

10. $(.9 - .043) + (6.3 - .09) =$ _____ (F)

| 11.6 | 25.38 | 7.067 | 25.38 | 10.84 | 5.774 | 15.353 |

| 7.067 | 14.293 | 11.6 | 10.84 | 3.65 |

| 84.85 | 10.84 | 15.353 |

| 15.353 | 19.91 | 10.84 |

BYE, UNCLE TUT!
HAVE A NICE TRIP!

Adding and subtracting decimals

NAME_____

Where does a tired artist sleep?

DIRECTIONS: Using the map below, answer each question. Each time your answer appears in the secret code, write the letter of the problem above it.

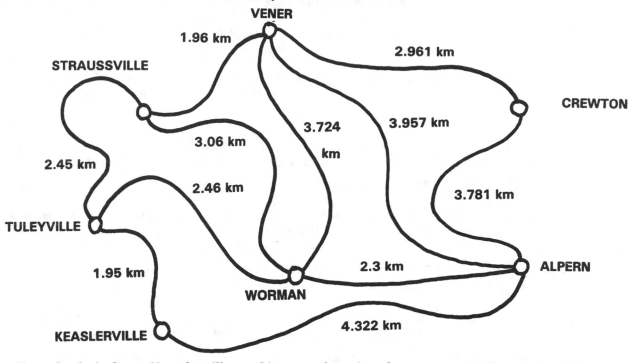

1.   How far is it from Keaslerville to Alpern using the shortest route ?_____(T)

2.   What is the total mileage from Vener→Worman→Tuleyville→Straussville?
      _____ (A)

3.   Which is farther: Alpern→Keaslerville→Tuleyville or Alpern→Worman→
      Tuleyville?_____How much farther?_____ (E)

4.   How far is it from Alpern →Straussville using the shortest route?_____ (N)

5.   Which is a shorter distance: Vener→Worman→Straussville →Vener or
      Alpern→Worman→Straussville →Vener?_____ How much shorter?
      _____ (P)

6.   If you rode your bike around the perimeter of the map, how far would you have
      ridden? _____ (L)

7.   The total mileage from Crewton→Alpern→Worman→Straussville is 9.141.   If you
      reached Worman by 2:00 PM, how much farther would you need to travel before you
      reached Straussville? _____ (O)

___ ___ ___ ___ ___ ___ ___ ___ ___

3.06   5.36   8.634   1.424   8.634   17.424   17.424   1.512   4.322

NAME_____

What is the title of this picture?

DIRECTIONS: To solve this puzzle, work each problem below on another sheet of paper. Each time your answer appears in the secret code, write the letter of the problem above it.

1. On a summer vacation trip, the Cooper family traveled the following distances: 121.3 miles, 234.5 miles, 482.9 miles, and 300 miles. How many total miles did the Cooper family travel? _____(G)

2. Lauren needed $18.20 to buy a new sweater. She earned $12.50 baby-sitting. How much more money did she need to earn to buy the sweater? _____(R)

3. During one year Atlanta had 53.2 inches of rainfall, and Nashville had 48.3 inches. How much more rainfall did Atlanta receive that year? _____ (O)

4. Shaun has four pieces of lumber which have the following lengths: 6.75 inches, 6.575 inches, 2.43 inches, and 7.125 inches. What is the total length of these pieces of wood? _____ (I)

5. Megan saw a sign in a jewelry store advertising a large diamond ring. The ring contained 3 separate diamonds. The center diamond weighed 2.08 carats, the diamond on the right of the center diamond weighed 1.83 carats, and the diamond on the left weighed 1.9 carats. What is the total weight of all the diamonds in this one ring? _____ (H)

6. A skier scored 234.8 points in ski jumping. Another skier scored 4.8 points higher. What was the second skier's score? _____ (S)

7. Janifer is 1.57 meters tall and Michelle is 1.39 meter tall. How much taller is Janifer than Michelle? _____ (M)

8. The gold medal for the Women's 100 Meter Dash in the 1960 Olympics was won by Wyomia Titus of the USA with a time of 11.49 seconds. The silver medal was won by Edith Maguire with a time of 11.62 seconds. How much faster was Wyomia's time? _____ (K)

9. Gary became sick at school, and his temperature rose from 98.6°F to 101.3°F in one hour's time. How many degrees did Gary's temperature rise? _____ (E)

_____	_____	_____	_____	_____	_____
2.7	239.6	.13	22.88	.18	4.9

_____	_____	_____	_____	_____	_____	_____	_____
5.81	22.88	1138.7	5.81	$5.70	22.88	239.6	2.7

NAME_____

Decimal Skill Test - Adding and subtracting

DIRECTIONS: Solve each problem on another sheet of paper. Put your answer in the space provided by each problem.

1. **2.474 + 75.84 =** _____   11. **52.7 - 6.4 =** _____

2. **6.0 + 5.02 + 7.004 =** _____   12. **.54 + 7.37 =** _____

3. **15.572 - 6.38 =** _____   13. **9.78 - 7.10 =** _____

4. **18.8 - 10.53 =** _____   14. **$6.75 + $.04 =** _____

5. **$67.89 - $67 .65 =** _____   15. **4.7 + 23 + 4.1 =** _____

6. **.765 + 3.876 + 5 =** _____   16. **6 - .08 =** _____

7. **.1 + .3 + 8.9 =** _____   17. **6 + .003 + .9 =** _____

8. **7.09 - 3.1 =** _____   18. **4.30 + .479 =** _____

9. **12 - 3.987 =** _____   19. **$56.73 - $1.07 =** _____

10. **6.4 + 3.89 + 2 + .009 =** _____ 20. **45 - 3.678 =** _____

SCORE _____

Multiplying decimals by 10, 100, 1000

28

NAME _____

Why do baby birds never smile?

DIRECTIONS: First, solve each of the problems on another sheet of paper. Second, find your answer in the secret code at the bottom of the page. Third, each time your answer appears in the secret code, write the letter of the problem above it.

To multiply by:	Move the decimal point to the right by:	
10	1 place or	4.270 x 10 = 42.7
100	2 places or	4.270 x 100 = 427.0
1000	3 places or	4.270 x 1000 = 4270

1. .86 x 10 = _____ (M)

2. .004 x 1000 = _____ (F)

3. 7.43 x 100 = _____ (W)

4. .65 x 100 = _____ (D)

5. 2.93 x 10 = _____ (N)

6. 37.843 x 1000 = _____ (R)

7. .9 x 100 = _____ (O)

8. 100 x 41.8 = _____ (I)

9. .878 x 100 = _____ (U)

10. 10 x 34.5 = _____ (L)

11. .0007 x 1000 = _____ (Y)

12. 1000 x .003 = _____ (E)

13. .91 x 1000 = _____ (S)

14. 1000 x .01 = _____ (T)

15. 3.4 x 10 = _____ (H)

___ ___ ___ ___ ___ ___ ___ ___ ___ ___ ___ ___
743 90   4   .7 90 87.8 345 90 87.8 65 37.843 .7

___ ___ ___ ___ ___ ___ ___ ___ ___ ___ ___
4,180 3   65   90 87.8 90 90 87.8 910   34 743

___ ___ ___ ___ ___ ___ ___ ___ ___ ___
4   3   29.3 345 90 4,180 8.6 37,843 90 910

___ ___ ___ ___ ___ ___ ___ ___
3   345 .7   8.6 37,843 910 8.6 3

Estimating decimal products

NAME_____

What's the richest country in the world?

DIRECTIONS: Estimate each product, and find your answer in the decoder. Each time the answer occurs in the decoder, write the letter of the problem above it.

1. 2.7 x 8.1 = _____ (S)

2. 5.2 x 22.8 = _____ (E)

3. $7.92 x 7.10 = _____(Y)

4. 3.89 x 56.12 = _____ (A)

5. .9 x 12.85 = _____ (P)

6. $9.36 x 8.9 = _____ (W)

7. $.78 x 3.95 = _____ (R)

8. 1.3 x 2.9 = _____ (D)

9. $15.86 x 3.9 = _____ (T)

10. 7.8 x 26.2 = _____ (L)

11. 9.298 x 3.841 = _____ (C)

12. 4.132 x 42.03 = _____ (U)

13. .8 x .91 = _____ (B)

14. 7.86 x 5.94 = _____(I)

15. $43.02 x 2.98 = _____ (N)

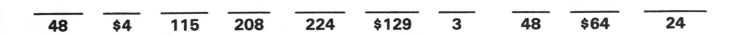

—									
48	$4	115	208	224	$129	3	48	$64	24

36	224	13	48	$64	224	208	48	24

224	208	$81	224	$56	24	3	168	1	208	48	$129

NAME_____

If you had only one tooth, what would you do?

DIRECTIONS: First, solve each of the problems on another sheet of paper. Second, find your answer in the secret code at the bottom of the page. Third, each time your answer appears in the secret code, write the letter of the problem above it.

1. $86.29 \times .73 =$ _____ **(D)**

2. $0.04 \times 1.4 =$ _____ **(N)**

3. $14.01 \times 39 =$ _____ **(T)**

4. $65.33 \times 29 =$ _____ **(E)**

5. $.342 \times .03 =$ _____ **(B)**

6. $.07 \times 46.38 =$ _____ **(I)**

7. $1.808 \times .35 =$ _____ **(R)**

8. $3.994 \times 6.7 =$ _____ **(G)**

9. $53.8 \times 2.14 =$ _____ **(A)**

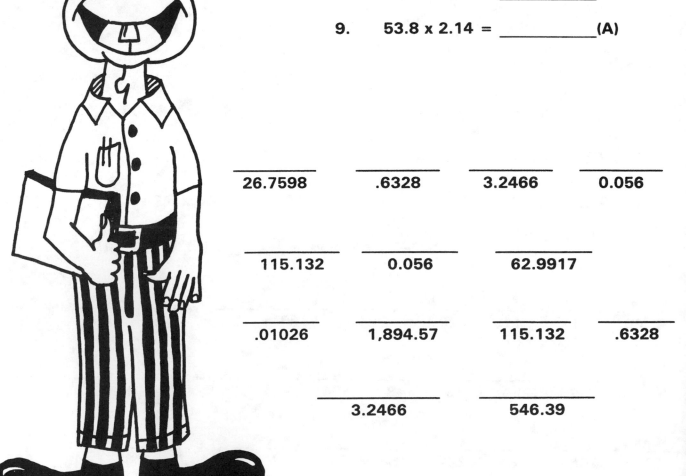

26.7598	.6328	3.2466	0.056

115.132	0.056	62.9917

.01026	1,894.57	115.132	.6328

3.2466	546.39

NAME_____

Trivia: What am I?

DIRECTIONS: To solve the trivia puzzles, work each problem below on another sheet of paper. Each time your answer appears in the secret code, write the letter of the problem above it.

1. I am a food that never spoils. I have been found in the old tombs of Egyptian rulers and, believe it or not, I still taste good.

2. I am the largest tree. I live in Sequoia National Park in California. I am 272 feet tall, and I weigh more than 2,000 pounds. I am named in honor of a famous Civil War general.

1. $4.2 \times 1.2 =$ _____ (M)   7. $29.3 \times 5.2 =$ _____ (Y)

2. $19.6 \times 4 =$ _____ (R)   8. $58.2 \times 5.71 =$ _____ (S)

3. $4.95 \times 0.9 =$ _____ (A)   9. $8.26 \times 472 =$ _____ (H)

4. $7.26 \times 1.2 =$ _____ (N)   10. $7.33 \times 4.26 =$ _____ (G)

5. $64.8 \times 4.6 =$ _____ (E)   11. $2.63 \times .747 =$ _____ (O)

6. $42.6 \times 0.48 =$ _____ (L)

1. _____ _____ _____ _____ _____ .

   3898.72   1.96461   8.712   298.08   152.36

2. _____ _____ _____ _____ _____ _____ _____

   31.2258   298.08   8.712   298.08   78.4   4.455   20.448

   _____ _____ _____ _____ _____ _____ _____

   332.322   3898.72   298.08   78.4   5.04   4.455   8.712

NAME_____

Decimal Skill Test - Multiplying

DIRECTIONS: Solve each problem on another sheet of paper. Put your answer in the space provided by each problem.

1.   16.3 x 5 = _____

2.   36 x .9 = _____

3.   63.4 x 0.7 = _____

4.   3.116 x 312 = _____

5. $3.66 x .54 = _____

6.   .87 x .009 = _____

7.   1000 x 1.234 = _____

8.   6.7 x 100 = _____

9.   2.3 x 2000 = _____

10. $56.24 x .14 = _____

11. 25.6 x 3.2 = _____

12. .25 x .3 = _____

13. .109 x 99 = _____

14. 43.35 x 2.7 = _____

15. 1.719 x 3.04 = _____

16. .008 x .0003 = _____

17. 3.24 x .9 = _____

18. 3.45 x 2.004 = _____

19. .9 x .8 = _____

20. 30 X .09 = _____

SCORE_____

Dividing decimals by 10, 100, 1,000, 10,000, and 100,000

How did the Eiffel Tower get its name?

DIRECTIONS: Solve each problem below. Each time your answer occurs in the decoder, write the letter of the problem above it.

1. $.75 \div 10 =$ _____ (H)

2. $634.8 \div 10 =$ _____ (P)

3. $9.4 \div 10 =$ _____ (E)

4. $7843 \div 1,000 =$ _____ (N)

5. $6.97 \div 100 =$ _____ (M)

6. $6,348 \div 100,000 =$ _____ (L)

7. $78.43 \div 100 =$ _____ (O)

8. $78.43 \div 10,000 =$ _____ (U)

9. $643.8 \div 1,000 =$ _____ (F)

10. $.75 \div 100 =$ _____ (R)

11. $6.97 \div 1,000 =$ _____ (Y)

12. $.94 \div 100 =$ _____ (G)

13. $431.9 \div 100 =$ _____ (A)

14. $4,319 \div 10 =$ _____ (T)

.6438	.00697	.94	431.9	.075	.94	431.9	63.48
.00697	.7843	.7843	.0697	.007843	.94	431.9	.7843	7.843
.0075	.7843	.007843	.0094	.94	.6438	.007843	4.319	.06348

Multiplying and dividing decimals by 10, 100 and 1,000

Why did the tightrope walker go to the bank?

NAME _____

REMEMBER: When multiplying decimals by multiples of ten, the decimal point is moved to the right.
When dividing decimals by multiples of ten, the decimal point is moved to the left.

DIRECTIONS: First, solve each problem below on another sheet of paper. Second, find your answer in the secret code at the bottom of the page. Third, each time your answer appears in the code, write the letter of the problem above it

1. .97 x 10 = _____ (N)

2. .034 ÷ 10 = _____ (O)

3. 1,000 x 7.43 = _____ (T)

4. 78.96 x 100 = _____ (D)

5. 1.342 ÷ 100 = _____ (B)

6. 4.971 x 1,000 = _____ (S)

7. 10 x 3.43 = _____ (A)

8. 1.342 x 10 = _____ (L)

9. 89.1 ÷ 1,000 = _____ (H)

10. 34 ÷ 100 = _____ (E)

11. 7.896 x 10 = _____ (K)

12. .343 ÷ 10 = _____ (W)

13. 497.1 ÷ 100 = _____ (C)

14. .891 x 100 = _____ (I)

| .0891 | .34 | .0343 | 34.3 | 9.7 | 7,430 | .34 | 4,971 | .01342 | 34.3 | 13.42 | 4.971 | .0891 | .34 | 4.971 | 78.96 |

| .0891 | 89.1 | 4,971 | 7,896 | .0034 | 7,430 | 4.971 | .0891 | 34.3 | 9.7 | 4.971 | .34 |

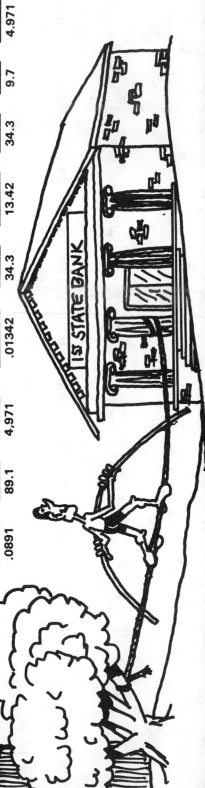

1ST STATE BANK

Problem Solving = Multiplying and dividing decimals

NAME_____

What is the title of this picture?

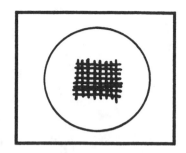

DIRECTIONS: To solve this puzzle, work each problem below on another sheet of paper. Each time your answer appears in the secret code, write the letter of the problem above it.

1. There are 26 children in Mrs. Cabrera's class. If 0.5 of the class went swimming, how many children went swimming? _____(U)

2. Pamela spent .7 of her pay she received for baby-sitting on a set of books about horses. If she earned $8.00, how much did she spend? _____ (O)

3. If the average speed of a jet plane is 625.52 miles per hour, how many total miles does the jet travel in 3.5 hours? _____ (T)

4. If super unleaded gasoline costs 98.5 cents per gallon, how much would 50 gallons cost? _____ (N)

5. For her Arabian costume, Amber needed 4.5 yards of material. The price of the fabric was $2.35 per yard. How much did Amber's mom spend for the fabric? _____ (E)

6. Mrs. Gray purchased a 15 lb. turkey for $12.75. What was the price of the turkey per pound? _____ (M)

7. In four successive weeks, Vanessa spent $2.25, $4.50, $.98 and $6.75 on her rock collections. What was the average cost per week for her hobby? _____(A)

8. Max and Austin hiked 5.25 miles one morning before taking a break. If they had been hiking for 3 hours, what was their average distance per hour? _____ (D)

_____	_____	_____	_____	_____	_____	_____
$3.62	$0.85	$10.58	$49.25	1.75	$10.58	1.75

_____	_____	_____	_____	_____
1.75	$5.60	$49.25	13	2,189.32

NAME _____

Dividing decimals by whole numbers

What was Noah's profession?

DIRECTIONS: Solve each problem below on another sheet of paper. Find your answer in the decoder at the bottom of the page. Each time your answer occurs in the decoder, write the letter of the problem

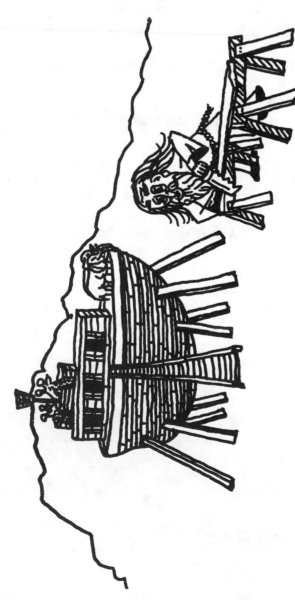

1. 20.34 ÷ 9 = _____ (T)

2. 23.52 ÷ 98 = _____ (C)

3. 198.66 ÷ 86 = _____ (I)

4. 58.422 ÷ 91 = _____ (E)

5. 157.56 ÷ 52 = _____ (R)

6. 27.768 ÷ 78 = _____ (K)

7. .0468 ÷ 9 = _____ (A)

$$\overline{.0052} \quad \overline{3.03} \quad \overline{0.356} \quad \overline{2.31} \quad \overline{2.26} \quad \overline{.642} \quad \overline{0.24} \quad \overline{2.26}$$

Why do dragons sleep in the morning and afternoon?

DIRECTIONS: First, solve each problem below on another sheet of paper. Second, find your answer in the secret code at the bottom of the page. Third, each time your answer appears in the code, write the letter of the problem above it.

1. 6.232 ÷ .82 = _____ (K)

2. 72.45 ÷ 4.5 = _____ (H)

3. 1.462 ÷ 3.4 = _____ (S)

4. 92.1 ÷ .03 = _____ (O)

5. 2.065 ÷ .35 = _____ (I)

6. 0.9345 ÷ .015 _____ (E)

7. 2.352 ÷ 4.2 = _____ (N)

8. 5.0752 ÷ 6.1 = _____ (U)

9. 1.84 ÷ .2 = _____ (L)

10. 48.64 ÷ .32 = _____ (G)

11. 4.656 ÷ 1.6 = _____ (Y)

12. 36 ÷ .6 = _____ (T)

$$\overline{60} \quad \overline{16.1} \quad \overline{62.3} \quad \overline{2.91} \quad \overline{16.1} \quad \overline{9.2} \quad \overline{5.9} \quad \overline{.56} \quad \overline{7.6} \quad \overline{62.3}$$

$$\overline{60} \quad \overline{3070} \quad \overline{5.9} \quad \overline{0.832} \quad \overline{.56} \quad \overline{60}$$

$$\overline{7.6} \quad \overline{.56} \quad \overline{152} \quad \overline{16.1} \quad \overline{60} \quad \overline{.43}$$

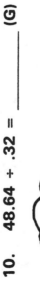

NAME _____

NAME_____

Prehistoric Trivia

DIRECTIONS: First, solve each problem below. Second, find your answer in the secret code at the bottom of the page. Third, each time your answer appears in the code, write the letter of the problem above it.

BACKGROUND INFORMATION: I was 36 feet long and twice as tall as an average human being. I had tremendous eyebrow horns which provided me with formidable protection from my larger dinosaur opponents by being lethal weapons. My huge plated neck shield also provided me with protection from the fatal bites of my larger enemies. What was I?

1. $92.1 \div .03 =$ _____ (C)

2. $11.655 \div 6.3 =$ _____ (O)

3. $196.62 \div 2.9 =$ _____ (E)

4. $1201.83 \div 41.3 =$ _____ (A)

5. $665.04 \div 13.6 =$ _____ (S)

6. $333.158 \div 10.6 =$ _____ (R)

7. $36 \div .6 =$ _____ (I)

8. $13.608 \div 5.5 =$ _____ (P)

9. $4.184 \div .08 =$ _____ (T)

| 52.3 | 31.43 | 60 | 3070 | 67.8 | 31.43 | 29.1 | 52.3 | 1.85 | 2.47 | 48.9 |

Dividing decimals

NAME_____

Decimal Skill Test - Dividing

DIRECTIONS: Solve each problem on another sheet of paper. Put your answer in the space provided by each problem. If you have a remainder, it will be necessary to round it to the nearest thousandth or to the nearest cent.

1. $5.04 \div 7 =$ _____

2. $11.655 \div 6.3 =$ _____

3. $\$6.44 \div .43 =$ _____

4. $4.884 \div 7.4 =$ _____

5. $\$78.95 \div 1.45 =$ _____

6. $.195 \div .3 =$ _____

7. $5.486 \div .4$ _____

8. $547.4 \div 7 =$ _____

9. $345.6 \div 10 =$ _____

10. $\$256.86 \div 2.56 =$ _____

11. $49.92 \div 3.2 =$ _____

12. $19.2 \div 32 =$ _____

13. $26.2 \div 4 =$ _____

14. $121.77 \div 2.7 =$ _____

15. $2.268 \div 81 =$ _____

16. $30.54 \div 15 =$ _____

17. $.9 \div 100 =$ _____

18. $\$3.98 \div .64 =$ _____

19. $5.0752 \div 6.1 =$ _____

20. $.8976 \div 1000 =$ _____

SCORE_____

NAME_____

Why was Cleopatra so negative?

DIRECTIONS: Solve each problem and find your answer in the decoder. Each time your answer occurs in the decoder, write the letter of the problem above it.

1. 9.32 ÷ .8 = _____ (T)

2. 64.32 x 100 = _____ (F)

3. 8.91 x 3.4 = _____ (I)

4. 7.48 ÷ .08 = _____ (H)

5. 54.3 ÷ 1,000 = _____ (A)

6. 7.96 ÷ .002 = _____ (E)

7. 44.32 x .61 = _____ (U)

8. 7 - .03 = _____ (L)

9. .934 x 10 = _____ (N)

10. .749 + 7 + .34 = _____ (Q)

11. (9.4 + .6) x (3.2 - 1) = _____ (S)

12. 78.84 x 1,000 = _____ (D)

13. (6.4 + 3.2) - (7.8 - 6.34) = _____ (W)

14. 30.06 - 6.06 = _____ (O)

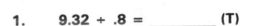

| 22 | 93.5 | 3,980 | 8.14 | .0543 | 22 | 11.65 | 93.5 | 3,980 |

| | 8.089 | 27.0352 | 3,980 | 3,980 | 9.34 |

| 24 | 6,432 | 78,840 | 3,980 | 9.34 | 30.294 | .0543 | 6.97 |

NAME_____

Using a calculator to change fractions to decimals

What is an archaeologist?

DIRECTIONS: Solve each problem with your calculator. If your answer is a repeating decimal, you will need to round your answer to the nearest thousandth. Each time your answer occurs in the decoder, write the letter of the problem above it.

1. $\frac{1}{3}$ = _____ (N)

2. $\frac{7}{12}$ = _____ (A)

3. $\frac{1}{22}$ = _____ (U)

4. $\frac{4}{27}$ = _____ (H)

5. $\frac{11}{12}$ = _____ (O)

6. $\frac{8}{9}$ = _____ (M)

7. $\frac{13}{15}$ = _____ (I)

8. $\frac{5}{20}$ = _____ (E)

9. $\frac{1}{50}$ = _____ (S)

10. $\frac{9}{11}$ = _____ (C)

11. $\frac{1}{6}$ = _____ (R)

12. $\frac{2}{3}$ = _____ (W)

$\overline{.02}$ $\overline{.917}$ $\overline{.889}$ $\overline{.25}$ $\overline{.917}$ $\overline{.333}$ $\overline{.25}$

$\overline{.667}$ $\overline{.148}$ $\overline{.917}$ $\overline{.02}$ $\overline{.25}$

$\overline{.818}$ $\overline{.583}$ $\overline{.167}$ $\overline{.25}$ $\overline{.25}$ $\overline{.167}$

$\overline{.867}$ $\overline{.02}$ $\overline{.867}$ $\overline{.333}$

$\overline{.167}$ $\overline{.045}$ $\overline{.867}$ $\overline{.333}$ $\overline{.02}$

Writing fractions as decimals

NAME _____

What do you call a cow with a newborn baby?

DIRECTIONS: First, divide to find the decimal for each fraction given below. Second, round the decimal to the nearest hundredth. Third, find your answer in the secret code, and write the letter of the problem above it.

1. $\dfrac{5}{6}$ = _____ (L)

2. $\dfrac{1}{13}$ = _____ (C)

3. $\dfrac{3}{20}$ = _____ (N)

4. $\dfrac{5}{8}$ = _____ (D)

5. $\dfrac{6}{7}$ = _____ (F)

6. $\dfrac{5}{9}$ = _____ (A)

7. $\dfrac{5}{11}$ = _____ (T)

8. $\dfrac{4}{9}$ = _____ (I)

9. $\dfrac{2}{3}$ = _____ (E)

.63 .08 .56 .83 .86 .44 .15 .56 .45 .67 .63

Writing fractions as decimals

NAME_____

Why is milk the fastest drink?

DIRECTIONS: First, calculate the decimal notation for each of the fractions below. Second, find your answer in the secret code at the bottom of the page. Third, each time your answer appears in the secret code, write the letter of the problem above it.

1. $\frac{1}{5}$ = _____(F)

2. $\frac{7}{10}$ = _____(T)

3. $3\frac{7}{25}$ = _____(R)

4. $5\frac{1}{4}$ = _____(E)

5. $2\frac{1}{2}$ = _____(P)

6. $8\frac{3}{5}$ = _____(D)

7. $11\frac{3}{4}$ = _____(S)

8. $\frac{9}{6}$ = _____(U)

9. $2\frac{7}{8}$ = _____(A)

10. $\frac{5}{6}$ = _____(Z)

11. $\frac{2}{8}$ = _____(I)

12. $\frac{1}{8}$ = _____(Y)

13. $\frac{1}{3}$ = _____(B)

14. $1\frac{6}{11}$ = _____(O)

| .25 | .7 | .25 | 11.75 |

| 2.5 | 2.875 | 11.75 | .7 | 5.25 | 1.5 | 3.28 | .25 | .833 | 5.25 | 8.6 |

| .333 | 5.25 | .2 | 1.545 | 3.28 | 5.25 |

| .125 | 1.545 | 1.5 |

| 11.75 | 5.25 | 5.25 |

| .25 | .7 |

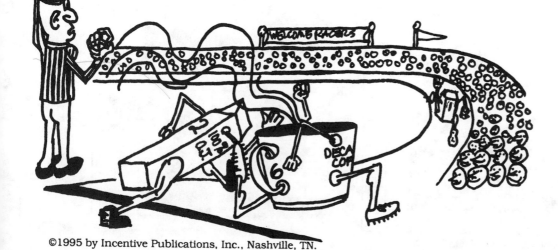

Using graphs to determine percents

What is another name for your funny bone?

NAME

DIRECTIONS: Find the percent of each graph that is shaded. Each time your answer occurs in the decoder, write the letter of the problem above it.

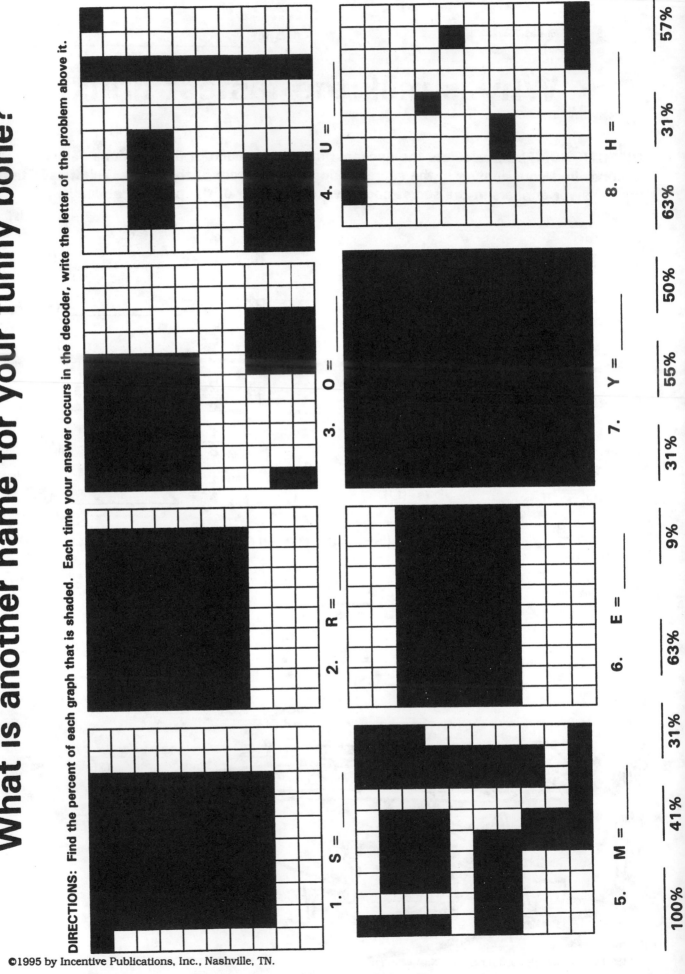

NAME_____

USING PERCENTS

DIRECTIONS: Think of the many, varied and unusual places or ways that percents are used in our daily lives. Try to think of at least ten.

1._____   8._____

2._____   9._____

3._____   10._____

4._____   11._____

5._____   12._____

6._____   13._____

7._____   14._____

EXTENSION ACTIVITY: Choose one of your examples of how percents are used and illustrate it.

NAME_____

Why did the cannibal stop eating humans?

DIRECTIONS: Write each decimal number as a percent. Then, find your answer in the secret code. Each time your answer appears in the secret code, write the letter of the problem above it.

1. .68 = _____ (D)

2. .3 = _____ (P)

3. .06 = _____ (L)

4. .94 = _____ (I)

5. 1.31 = _____ (W)

6. .53 = _____ (G)

7. .9 = _____ (T)

8. 2.54 = _____ (F)

9. .01 = _____ (E)

10. 1.58 = _____ (H)

11. .5 = _____ (O)

12. .43 = _____ (U)

| ‾‾‾ | ‾‾‾ | | ‾‾‾ | ‾‾‾ | ‾‾‾ |
| 158% | 1% | | 53% | 50% | 90% |

| ‾‾‾ | ‾‾‾ | ‾‾‾ | | ‾‾‾ | ‾‾‾ |
| 254% | 1% | 68% | | 43% | 30% |

| ‾‾‾ | ‾‾‾ | ‾‾‾ | ‾‾‾ |
| 131% | 94% | 90% | 158% |

| ‾‾‾ | ‾‾‾ | ‾‾‾ | ‾‾‾ | ‾‾‾ | ‾‾‾ |
| 30% | 1% | 50% | 30% | 6% | 1% |

Why is a rooster on a fence like a penny?

DIRECTIONS: Change each decimal to a percent. Find your answer in the decoder below, and each time your answer occurs, write the letter of the problem above it. (It will be necessary to round some problems to the nearest hundredth in order to determine the percent.)

1. .7 = _____ (N)

2. .54 = _____ (O)

3. .024 = _____ (L)

4. 1.34 = _____ (R)

5. .6 = _____ (S)

6. .093 = _____ (I)

7. .549 = _____ (H)

8. .2 = _____ (E)

9. .06 = _____ (D)

10. .746 = _____ (T)

11. .125 = _____ (A)

| 55% | 9% | 60% | | 55% | 20% | 13% | 6% | 9% | 60% |

| 54% | 70% | 54% | 70% | 20% | | 60% | 9% | 6% | 20% |

| 13% | 70% | 6% | 55% | 9% | 60% | | 75% | 13% | 9% | 2% |

| 54% | 70% | 75% | 55% | 20% | | 54% | 75% | 55% | 20% | 134% |

Writing percents as decimals

What did the honeydew melon say after the watermelon proposed marriage?

DIRECTIONS: Write each percent as a decimal. Then, find your answer in the secret code. Each time your answer appears in the secret code, write the letter of the problem above it.

1.   13% = _____ (N)

2.   30% = _____ (P)

3.   67% = _____ (Y)

4.   8% = _____ (L)

5.   28% = _____ (C)

6.   90% = _____ (U)

7.   43% = _____ (W)

8.   300% = _____ (E)

9.   9% = _____ (B)

10.   85% = _____ (O)

11.   250% = _____ (T)

12.   70% = _____ (A)

13.   2% = _____ (I)

14.   120% = _____ (S)

___ ___ ___   ___ ___ ___   ___
.67 3.0 1.2   .09 .9 2.5   .02

___ ___ ___ ___   ___ ___ ___ ___ ___ ___
.28 .7 .13 2.5   .7 .08 .85 .9 .3 3.0

___ ___ ___
.13 .85 .43

NAME_____

What makes doctors angry?

DIRECTIONS: Write each percent as a fraction in simplest form. Then, find your answer in the decoder. Each time your answer appears in the decoder, write the letter of the problem above it.

1.   31% = _____ (G)

2.   74% = _____ (F)

3.   35% = _____ (T)

4.   60% = _____ (U)

5.   2%   = _____ (I)

6.   76% = _____ (N)

7.   132% = _____ (O)

8.   55% = _____ (P)

9.   20% = _____ (E)

10. 167% = _____ (R)

11. 68% = _____ (A)

12. 26% = _____ (S)

$\frac{167}{100}$ $\frac{3}{5}$ $\frac{19}{25}$ $\frac{19}{25}$ $\frac{1}{50}$ $\frac{19}{25}$ $\frac{31}{100}$

$\frac{33}{25}$ $\frac{3}{5}$ $\frac{7}{20}$ $\frac{33}{25}$ $\frac{37}{50}$

$\frac{11}{20}$ $\frac{17}{25}$ $\frac{7}{20}$ $\frac{1}{50}$ $\frac{1}{5}$ $\frac{19}{25}$ $\frac{7}{20}$ $\frac{13}{50}$

Changing fractions to percents

NAME_____

ANIMALMANIA

DIRECTIONS: Change each fraction to a percent. Write your answer in the space provided. Each time your answer appears in the secret code, write the letter of the problem above it.

RIDDLES:

1. I am the world's smallest and most ferocious mammal. I have a bite like a cobra and eat twice my own weight in meat every day. I can attack and be victorious over an animal three times my size. What am I?

2. I am an insect that most people think has wings and can fly, but I can't. However, I can jump one hundred times my own height. Also, I can be very dangerous because I suck the blood of my host. I especially like the blood of dogs, cats, rodents, or even you. What am I?

3. I am the most ferocious and deadly fish. I have teeth as sharp as razor blades. However, I never attack alone, but as part of a school. No animal of any size can survive if my friends and I attack as a team. What am I?

1. $\frac{12}{20}$ = _____ (R)

2. $\frac{4}{8}$ = _____ (H)

3. $\frac{3}{12}$ = _____ (W)

4. $\frac{9}{10}$ = _____ (I)

5. $\frac{7}{35}$ = _____ (A)

6. $\frac{4}{5}$ = _____ (L)

7. $\frac{12}{16}$ = _____ (E)

8. $\frac{16}{40}$ = _____ (S)

9. $\frac{7}{10}$ = _____ (N)

10. $\frac{27}{90}$ = _____ (P)

11. $\frac{33}{33}$ = _____ (F)

1.

    40%   50%   60%   75%   25%

2. _____ _____ _____ _____

    100%   80%   75%   20%

3.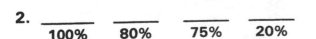

    30%   90%   60%   20%   70%   50%   20%

Writing ratios as percents

NAME_____

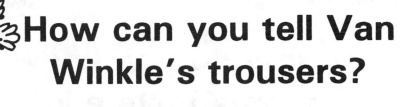

How can you tell Van Winkle's trousers?

DIRECTIONS: Percent means "per hundred." You can think of percent as a ratio that compares a number to 100. Write each ratio as a percent. Each time your answer occurs in the decoder, write the letter of the problem above it.

1. The AMC Theater had 100 seats and 57 of them were filled. What percent were filled? _____ (H)

2. 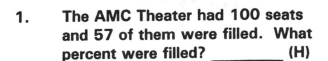 $\frac{32}{100}$ = _____ (W)

3. .22 = _____ (S)

4. 78 to 100 = _____ (Y)

5. 51 : 100 = _____ (M)

6. If a film festival showed 100 films, and 11 were directed by Steven Spielberg, what percent of the films were not directed by Spielberg? _____ (E)

7. 17 out of 100 = _____ (A)

8. .08 = _____ (O)

9. If there were 100 runners in the track meet, and 11 of them received medals, what percent received medals? _____ (N)

10. If you had 100 pennies, and you loaned 15 to your friend, what percent would you still have? _____ (I)

11. 6 : 100 = _____ (T)

12. 79 to 100 = _____ (P)

13. .33 = _____ (R)

___	___	___	___	___	___	___	___	___
6%	57%	89%	78%	33%	89%	6%	57%	89%

___	___	___	___	___	___	___	___	___
8%	11%	89%	22%	32%	85%	6%	57%	17%

___	___	___	___	___	___	___	___	___
33%	85%	79%	85%	11%	6%	57%	89%	51%

Finding the percentage of a number

NAME_____

How do you know that Army sergeants have a lot of headaches?

DIRECTIONS: Solve each problem below. Each time your answer occurs in the decoder, write the letter of the problem above it.

1. 85% of 94 = _____ (W)

2. 57% of .7 = _____ (S)

3. 26% of 40 = _____ (H)

4. 98% of .16 = _____ (Y)

5. 23.5% of 11 = _____ (A)

6. 3% of 346 = _____ (E)

7. 9% of 114 = _____ (I)

8. 5% of 98 = _____ (O)

9. 80% of 36 = _____ (L)

10. 38% of 95 = _____ (T)

11. 1% of 1 = _____ (N)

$\overline{\text{36.1}}$ $\overline{\text{10.4}}$ $\overline{\text{10.38}}$ $\overline{\text{.1568}}$ $\overline{\text{2.585}}$ $\overline{\text{28.8}}$ $\overline{\text{79.9}}$ $\overline{\text{2.585}}$ $\overline{\text{.1568}}$ $\overline{\text{.399}}$

$\overline{\text{.1568}}$ $\overline{\text{10.38}}$ $\overline{\text{28.8}}$ $\overline{\text{28.8}}$ $\overline{\text{36.1}}$ $\overline{\text{10.38}}$ $\overline{\text{.01}}$ $\overline{\text{.399}}$ $\overline{\text{10.26}}$ $\overline{\text{4.9}}$ $\overline{\text{.01}}$

What rock group kills household germs?

DIRECTIONS: First, solve each of the problems on another sheet of paper. Second, find your answer in the secret code at the bottom of the page. Third, each time your answer appears in the secret code, write the letter of the problem above it.

1. 5% of 34 = _____ (C)   6. 26% of 40 = _____ (A)

2. 8% of 720 = _____ (E)   7. 65% of 20 = _____ (O)

3. 30% of 120 = _____ (Y)   8. 9% of 114 = _____ (T)

4. 55% of 480 = _____ (H)   9. 8% of 96 = _____ (L)

5. 25% of 4 = _____ (S)   10. 26% of 85 = _____ (B)

_____ _____ _____
  10.26   264   57.6

_____ _____ _____ _____ _____ _____
  22.1   7.68   57.6   10.4   1.7   264

_____ _____ _____ _____
  22.1   13   36   1

NAME_____

Percentage Skill Test

Write as a percent.

1. .73 = _____

2. .04 = _____

3. .09 = _____

4. .3 = _____

5. 1.30 = _____

Write as a decimal.

6. 69% = _____

7. 7% = _____

8. 80% = _____

9. 175% = _____

10. 270% = _____

Write each percent as a fraction in simplest form.

11. 35% = _____

12. 2% = _____

13. 132% = _____

14. 26% = _____

15. 11 % = _____

Write each fraction as a percent.

16. $\frac{3}{4}$ = _____

17. $\frac{4}{25}$ = _____

18. $\frac{2}{5}$ = _____

19. $\frac{21}{10}$ = _____

20. $\frac{3}{10}$ = _____

Find the percent of each number.

21. 4% of 200 = _____

22. 50% of 44 = _____

23. 95% of 60 = _____

24. 5% of 710 = _____

25. 40% of 160 = _____

SCORE_____

NAME_____

What is a lunatic blackbird?

DIRECTIONS: Using your calculator, solve each problem. Locate your answer in the decoder, and each time your answer occurs, write the letter of the problem above it.

1.   78% of 1,100 = _____ **(C)**

2.   8% of 800 = _____ **(R)**

3.   65% of 120 = _____ **(I)**

4.   125% of 84 = _____ **(A)**

5.   If you had a test with 60 questions and you answered 80% correctly, how many questions did you answer correctly? _____ **(V)**

6.   If you were paying for a saxophone that retails for $3,200 and you paid 75% of this price, how much <u>more</u> do you need to pay? _____ **(M)**

7.   If the Pittsburg Pirates had played 80% of their 160 scheduled games, how many <u>more</u> games remain in the season? _____ **(E)**

8.   Ryan's swimming club planned a white water rafting trip during summer vacation. Only 70% of the club went on the trip. If there were 40 club members, how many swimmers went on the trip? _____ **(N)**

| 64 | 105 | 48 | 32 | 28 | $800.00 | 105 | 28 | 78 | 105 | 858 |

Finding the percentage of a number

NAME_____

What do you call a cow that can't give milk?

DIRECTIONS: First, solve each problem below on another sheet of paper. Second, find your answer in the secret code. Each time your answer appears in the secret code, write the letter of the problem above it.

1. **65% of 20 = _____ (L)**

2. **8% of 525 = _____ (E)**

3. **70% of 20 = _____ (R)**

4. **55% of 480 = _____ (D)**

5. **25% of 212 = _____ (A)**

6. On a school class trip to the mountains, only 70% of the class was able to go. If there were 30 people in the class, how many students went on the trip?_____ **(N)**

7. A European vacation for two was advertised for $1,400. If David and Gary had earned 60% of the amount they needed, how much had they earned?_____ **(I)**

8. If there were 60 problems on a math test and Dani got 90% of the problems correct, how many problems did she answer correctly? _____ **(U)**

9. Jenny wants to buy a car that costs $18,500. She needs a down payment of 20%. How much will the down payment be? _____ **(F)**

__	__		__	__	__	__	__
53	21		54	264	264	42	14

__	__	__	__	__	__	__
3,700	53	840	13	54	14	42

Land Area of Continents

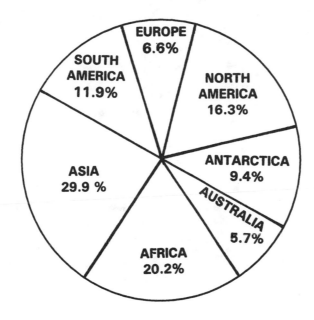

DIRECTIONS: Using the circle graph above, answer the following questions.

1. Which is the smallest continent? _____

2. Which continent is bigger, Europe or Antarctica? _____

3. Which continent takes up about 1/5 of the world's land surface? _____

4. Which continent takes up about 1/6 of the world's land surface?_____

5. The combined area of Europe and Australia is about the same as the area of which
    continent? _____

6. Which is larger, the combination of Africa, Australia, and Antarctica, or Asia?

    _____

EXTENSION OR EXTRA CREDIT: Rank the 10 most populous countries in the world in order
                               using percentages. Consult the most recent World Almanac.

NAME _____

Using higher order thinking skills to design a metric collage

My Metric Collage

DIRECTIONS: Create a metric collage by gluing clippings or labels from newspapers, magazines, canned foods, bottles, etc. You should have at least ten items showing examples of meters, liters, and grams.

Measuring line segments using metric notation

NAME _____

METRIC CASTLE

DIRECTIONS: Using the drawing of the metric castle, measure the following line segments, and round your answer to the nearest centimeter. Put your rounded answers in the spaces provided. The first one has been done for you. The answers are in mixed order on the left side of your paper. You may have the same answer for two problems.

ANSWERS

a. 18 cm
b. 10 cm
c. 15 cm
d. 3 cm
e. 9 cm
f. 12 cm
g. 6 cm
h. 3 cm
i. 9 cm
j. 23 cm
k. 11 cm

1. $\overline{AB}$ = 19 cm

2. $\overline{CD}$ =

3. $\overline{EF}$ =

4. $\overline{GH}$ =

5. $\overline{JK}$ =

6. $\overline{GL}$ =

7. $\overline{MN}$ =

8. $\overline{CL}$ =

9. $\overline{EL}$ =

10. $\overline{AL}$ =

11. $\overline{AH}$ =

12. $\overline{LN}$ =

EXTENSION: Use the metric castle drawing as a guide for designing a futuristic space station. Label 10-15 points with alphabet letters as is done on the metric castle. Then choose and write on another sheet of paper 10-15 line segments for a friend to measure. You may want to add color to your space station drawing. See page 61.

NAME

Using higher order thinking skills with metrics

METRIC CASTLE

NAME _____

SPACE STATION

Use the metric castle drawing as a guide for designing a futuristic space station. Label 10-15 points with alphabet letters as is done in the metric castle.

Problem solving with metrics

NAME_____

Metric Art Gallery of Miniatures

DIRECTIONS: In the frames provided below, draw 10 to 20 objects which measure five centimeters or less.

NAME_____

Metrics Scavenger Hunt

DIRECTIONS: In your school or home environment, find objects that will fit into each category given below.

Objects that measure about 5 centimeters

1. _____

2. _____

Objects that measure 1-5 millimeters

1. _____

2. _____

Objects that measure about 1 meter

1. _____

2. _____

Objects that weigh about 1-5 grams

1. _____

2. _____

Objects that hold about 10 milliliters

1. _____

2. _____

Objects that hold about 500 milliliters

1. _____

2. _____

Objects that hold about 1 liter

1. _____

2. _____

Objects that hold over 100 liters

1. _____

2. _____

Objects that weigh about 1 kilogram

1. _____   2. _____

NAME_____

Metrics: Making the right choice

DIRECTIONS: For each item listed, choose the measurement from the list in each of the three boxes. Write your answer in the space provided.

Measurement of Length:
meter, millimeter, centimeter, kilometer

---

1. the length of a tennis shoe _____

2. the length of a straw _____

3. the height of an oak tree _____

4. the distance a plane flies in a day _____

5. the length of your desk _____

6. the width of your desk _____

7. the length of an ant _____

8. the distance from Atlanta, GA, to Dallas, TX _____

9. the length of a fingernail _____

10. the width of a shoelace _____

11. the distance from Jupiter to Earth _____

Liquid Measurement:
liter, milliliter

Measurement of Weight:
gram, milligram, kilogram

---

12. a carton of school milk _____

13. a laboratory test tube _____

14. an aquarium _____

15. a medicine dropper _____

16. a car gas tank_____

17. a bathtub _____

18. a raindrop _____

19. an aspirin tablet_____

20. a feather _____

21. a rhinoceros _____

22. a sewing needle _____

23. a television _____

24. a snowflake _____

25. an egg _____

Which weighs more, a ton of feathers or a ton of lead?

DIRECTIONS: Solve each problem and find your answer in the decoder. Each time your answer occurs in the decoder, write the answer of the problem above it. Below is a rhyme that might help you remember whether to multiply or divide when converting decimal numbers .

Big to small, multiply all;
small to big, divide the pig.
Example:

$3 m = \underline{3,000} mm$ $3 \times 1000 = 3,000 mm$

$3 mm = \underline{.003} m$ $3 \div 1,000 = .003 m$

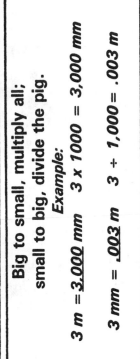

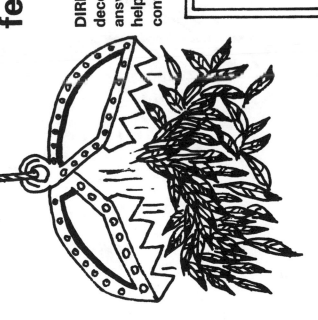

1. 7 km = _____ m (E)

2. 3.5 L = _____ mL (B)

3. 6.35 kg = _____ g (I)

4. 8.25 km = _____ m (A)

5. 70 cm = _____ mm (H)

6. .29 L = _____ mL (S)

7. 8 kg = _____ g (O)

8. 4.32 g = _____ mg (M)

9. .045 L = _____ mL (T)

10. .97 cm = _____ mm(G)

11. .035 L = _____ mL (Y)

12. .825 km = _____ m (W)

—— —— —— —— —— —— —— —— ——
45 700 7,000 35 3,500 8,000 700 45 825 6,350 9.7 700

—— —— —— —— ——
45 700 7,000 290 8,250 4,320 7,000

Dividing to change metric units

When is music like an icy pavement?

DIRECTIONS: First, solve each problem below on another sheet of paper. Second, find your answer in the secret code at the bottom of the page. Third, each time your answer appears in the code, write the letter of the problem above it.

REMEMBER: When dividing a decimal by 10, 100, or 1,000, the decimal point is moved to the left.

1. 7 mm = ___ m (I)
2. 3 m = ___ km (F)
3. 12,600 m = ___ km (T)
4. 5,000 mm = ___ m (D)
5. 705 cm = ___ m (H)
6. 47.6 mm = ___ cm (Y)

7. 8,000 m = ___ km (L)
8. 4,300 cm = ___ m (O)
9. 766 cm = ___ m (A)
10. 98 mm = ___ cm (N)
11. 80,000 m = ___ km (U)
12. .4 mm = ___ m (W)

13. .09 mm = ___ cm (E)
14. 3,900 mm = ___ cm (C)
15. .03 m = ___ km (P)
16. 9,000 m = ___ km (B)
17. 785 cm = ___ m (R)
18. .85 cm = ___ m (S)

.0004 7.05 .009 9.8

4.76 43 80

.0004 .007 8

9 .003 8 7.66 12.6

.007 .003 4.76 43 80

5 43 9.8 12.6 390

.0085 7.05 7.66 7.85 .00003

NAME_____

Why does lightning shock people?

DIRECTIONS: First, solve each problem below. Second, find your answer in the secret code at the bottom of the page. Third, each time your answer appears in the code, write the letter of the problem above it.

1. 12 m = _____ km (E)

2. 4 km = _____ m (W)

3. .387 cm = _____ mm (S)

4. 6004 m = _____ km (D)

5. 10 L = _____ mL (K)

6. 357 m = _____ km (L)

7. .56 L = _____ mL (H)

8. .079 L = _____ mL (I)

9. .14 g = _____ mg (U)

10. .01 g = _____ mg (C)

11. 1.3 kg = _____ g (O)

12. .035 kg = _____ g (F)

13. 7 mm = _____ cm (T)

14. .426 cm = _____ mm (N)

__	__	__	__	__	__	__	__
79	.7	6.004	1,300	.012	3.87	4.26	.7

__	__	__	__
10,000	4.26	1,300	4,000

__	__	__	__	__
560	1,300	4,000	.7	1,300

__	__	__	__	__	__	__
10	1,300	4.26	6.004	140	10	.7

__	__	__	__	__	__
79	.7	3.87	.012	.357	35

NAME_____

METRIC SKILL TEST

DIRECTIONS: Give the best metric measurement for each of the objects listed below.

Length - meter, millimeter, centimeter,

1. the length of the chalkboard _____

2. the length of your math book _____

3. the diameter of a needle _____

4. the distance from Venus to the Sun _____

Liquid - liter, milliliter

5. a drinking glass _____

6. a thimble _____

7. a teaspoon _____

8. a swimming pool_____

Weight - gram, milligram, kilogram

9. an adult person _____

10. a blade of grass _____

11. a telephone _____

12. an ice cream bar _____

DIRECTIONS: Multiply or divide to change metric units.

13. 6 L = _____ mL

14. .389 cm = _____ mm

15. 95 cm = _____ m

16. 49 km = _____ m

17. 7.003 km = _____ m

18. 48 g = _____ mg

19. 358 mL = _____ L

20. 27 km = _____ m

21. 29.3 g = _____ kg

22. 8 g = _____ kg

23. .92 L = _____ mL

24. 34 mg = _____ g

25. 780 mg = _____ g

SCORE_____

NAME_____

Hot or Cold?

Directions: Using the Celsius thermometer, circle the more suitable temperature for:

1. skateboarding   27°C   80°C

2. building a snowman   -3°C   32°C

3. heating a bowl of soup   0°C   100°C

4. flying a kite   76°C   29°C

5. sitting in a hot tub   13°C   40°C

6. going swimming   30°C   85°C

7. freezing popsicles   20°C   0°C

8. planting flowers   75°C   25°C

9. skiing in the snow   2°C   30°C

10. snorkeling in the Caribbean   25°C   79°C

11. camping in the woods   22°C   76°C

12. playing a game of baseball   26°C   75°C

13. visiting Antarctica   –30°C   15°C

14. going boating   85°C   28°C

15. riding a dune buggy at the beach   40°C   82°C

Using a calculator to plan a budget

NAME_____

It's Budget Time

DIRECTIONS: John has just rented his own apartment. He knows he will need to be careful with *how* he spends his money because he must be able to pay all of his monthly bills. Using your calculator, help John determine what percent of his monthly paycheck each of the following will be:

Monthly Paycheck: $1580.00

```
Nº 687          GERALD S. FOWLER CO.        50-226
                ANYPLACE, N.Y. 00055          213

                                DEC. 31, 19 95

PAY TO THE    JOHN RODGERS              $1580.00
ORDER OF _____
ONE THOUSAND FIVE HUNDRED + EIGHTY 00/100 DOLLARS
   BLANK BANK
   ANYPLACE, N.Y. 00055            Gerald S. Fowler

⑈021302268⑈ 1234⑈07889⑈  0687  ⑈00000102954⑈
```

Percent of paycheck

Apartment Rent	$550.00	_____
Utilities	$210.00	_____
Car Payment	$256.00	_____
School Loan Payment	$85.00	_____
Food/Gas	$350.00	_____

What is the total percent of all his bills? _____

What percent does John have left for entertainment? _____

Extension: As a class project, decide on a given amount of money and plan a budget for your class or home.

Checking accuracy of bank account

Balanced Books

DIRECTIONS: Mrs. Consumer has difficulty keeping her account balanced. See if you can help her out. Her current balance is given and all of her transactions for the month are listed.

Transactions for March:

Current Balance: $758.23

Deposits

Date	Amount
3-2	$550.00
3-14	$1,654.15
3-25	$3,462.23

Checks Written

Check #	Date	Amount
1206	3-1	$406.12
1207	3-3	$216.95
1208	3-10	$67.05
1209	3-15	$972.54
1210	3-16	$5.61
1211	3-17	$25.00
1212	3-20	$515.12
1213	3-27	$2,986.14
1214	3-29	$162.19

Date	Check Number	Amount of Check	Amount of Deposit	Balance
			Current Balance:	

NAME_____

Why was Adam the fastest runner?

DIRECTIONS: Find the sale price of each of the following using what you have learned by percentages. After you solved each problem on another sheet of paper, find your answer in the decoder and place the letter of the problem above it.

	Regular price	Discount	Sale Price	
1.	$9.50	10%	_____	(A)
2.	$10.00	20%	_____	(R)
3.	$4.00	25%	_____	(C)
4.	$7.80	25%	_____	(N)
5.	$6.00	30%	_____	(E)
6.	$7.50	50%	_____	(S)
7.	$16.00	5%	_____	(T)
8.	$12.00	40%	_____	(F)
9.	$11.00	25%	_____	(I)
10.	$36.00	60%	_____	(M)
11.	$75.00	75%	_____	(W)
12.	$20.00	40%	_____	(H)
13.	$15.90	20%	_____	(U)

$12.00	$4.20	$18.75	$8.55	$3.75	$15.20	$12.00	$4.20

$7.20	$8.25	$8.00	$3.75	$15.20	$8.25	$5.85	$15.20	$12.00	$4.20

$12.00	$12.72	$14.40	$8.55	$5.85	$8.00	$8.55	$3.00	$4.20

Problem solving - Percentages and discounts

NAME_____

Newspaper Scavenger Hunt For Sales

Daily News

For Sale
Baseball Bat
25% Off
Was $12.75 Now $9.56

DIRECTIONS: In your school or home environment, find objects that will fit into each category given below.

Name of Item	Regular Price	Percentage of Discount	Amount of Discount	Sale Price
1. Baseball bat	$12.75	25%	$3.19	$9.56
2.				
3.				
4.				
5.				
6.				
7.				
8.				
9.				
10.				

In this space place the newspaper ad you think promotes the best deal for the consumer.

NAME_____

What is the title of this picture?

DIRECTIONS: To solve this puzzle, work each problem below on another sheet of paper. Each time your answer appears in the secret code, write the letter of the problem above it.

1. About 65% of the human body is water. About 70% of an elephant's body is water, and an earthworm's body is composed of 80% water. What percentage of a human's body is not water? _____ **(M)**

2. If Joey made 12 baskets out of 24 shots, what percent of the baskets did he make? _____ **(R)**

3. On a test Catherine answered 36 out of 40 questions correctly. What percent of the questions did she get correct? _____ **(N)**

4. A $65.00 skateboard is on sale at a 20% discount. Find the savings. _____ **(G)**

5. If 70% is passing on a math test, how many problems on a 40 question test will Lauren need to get correct in order to pass the test? _____ **(O)**

6. If a state has a 5% sales tax, how much tax would be charged on a $300.00 purchase? _____ **(I)**

7. If Ben wants to pay a down payment of 24% on a $300.00 bicycle, how much money must he pay down? _____ **(F)**

8. In the election for class secretary, Andrea received 20 of the 25 votes cast. What percentage of the votes did she receive? _____ **(A)**

9. If a television set regularly priced at $500.00 is on sale at a discount of 40%, what is the price of the TV? _____ **(P)**

10. If Christian has made 13 hits out of his 39 times at bat, what is his batting average in decimal notation? _____ **(E)**

_____	_____	_____
$300.00	$15.00	$13.00

_____	_____	_____	_____	_____	_____	_____	_____
.333	35%	.333	50%	$13.00	$15.00	90%	$13.00

_____	_____	_____	_____	_____	_____	_____	_____
$72.00	50%	28	35%	80%	$72.00	28	$13.00

BRAIN CHALLENGERS:

DECIMALS, PERCENTAGES, METRIC SYSTEM AND CONSUMER MATH

NAME_____

Why did the lazy man want to work in a bakery?

DIRECTIONS: Use the numbers 1-9 to solve the problems below. As you solve each problem, write the letter for each number in the decoder. Show your work on another sheet of paper. *Clue: Everytime there's an A, replace it with a 3.*

1.
```
  LE.R
x   A
-----
  EA.R
```

2.
```
  WE.A
x    O
-----
 LSW.S
```

3.
```
   OA.E
   RH.W
+   H.L
------
  WW.A
```

4.
```
  LL.RS
x    E
------
  ES.OE
```

5.
```
  AE.WR
- H.AS
------
  OH.EF
```

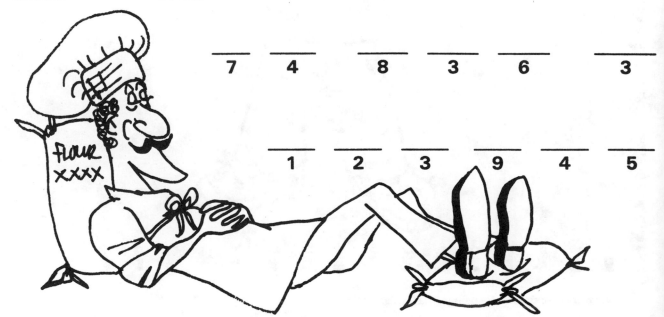

```
  7   4   8   3   6   3
 ___ ___ ___ ___ ___ ___

  1   2   3   9   4   5
 ___ ___ ___ ___ ___ ___
```

Analysis and synthesis

THINKING WORDS
combine, integrate, relate

NAME _____

Which way did the cowboy computer programmer go?

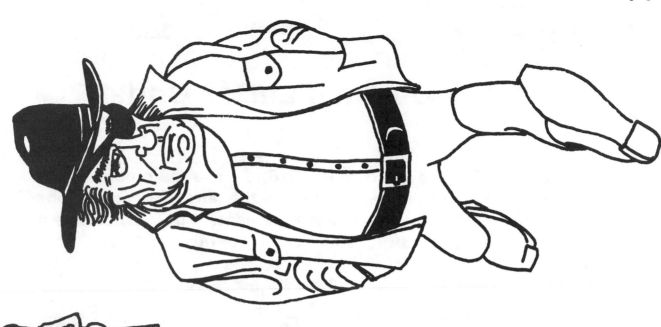

DIRECTIONS: Use the clues given in each problem to discover the mystery decimal number.

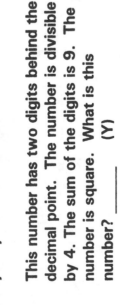

1. This number has two digits behind the decimal point. The number is divisible by 4. The sum of the digits is 9. The number is square. What is this number? _____ (Y)

2. This number has one digit in front and one behind the decimal point. The number is square. The product of the digits is divisible by 8. The sum of the digits is even. What is this number? _____ (D)

3. This number has two digits behind the decimal point. It is divisible by 6. The sum of the digits is divisible by 5. The product of the digits is divisible by 4. What is this number? _____ (A)

4. This number has one digit in front and two digits behind the decimal point. The number is square. The sum of the digits is divisible by 3. The product of the digits is divisible by 4. The sum of the digits is 9. What is this number? _____ (W)

5. This number has one digit in front and one digit behind the decimal point. The sum of the digits is divisible by 6 and when added together is a multiple of 6. The number is greater than five and less than 10. What is this number? _____ (T)

| 6.4 | .78 | 8.4 | .78 | 1.44 | .78 | .36 |

Analysis and synthesis

NAME _____

Decimal Letter Code

DIRECTIONS: Use the numbers 1-8 to solve the problems below on a separate sheet of paper. Then place the letter for each number in the decoder below to complete the statement. **HINT:** There are no zeros in the problems, and the letter "C" = the number 1.

1.
```
  CA.T
x    E
─────
  AE.T
```

2.
```
  YA.E
x    R
─────
  CIY.I
```

3.
```
  CC.TI
x     A
──────
  AI.RA
```

4.   I.A ÷ Y = .Y

5.   Y.A ÷ I = C.A

6.
```
  RE.A
  TV.Y
+ V.C
─────
  YY .E
```

THINKING WORDS

infer

generate

reconstruct

To solve this letter code, you must use a lot of

___ ___ ___ ___ ___ ___ ___ ___ ___ ___
 1   2   3   4   5   6   7   6   5   8

NAME_____

A Maze of Decimals

DIRECTIONS: Move through this maze as fast as you can from start (1) to finish (5.5). You may move one square in any direction, but you can only move to a number that is 1.6 *more* or 2.3 *less* than the number you are on.

THINKING WORDS

compute

apply

calculate

combine

relate

Start here					
1	2.4	.3	3.6	2.8	.7
1.6	2.6	4.1	1.9	4.3	-1.6
3.1	1.3	-.4	1.3	2.4	3.2
3.6	1.2	1.8	2.0	-1.3	2.8
4.2	.7	2.8	.5	4.2	3.6
3.1	2.3	1.4	2.1	1.9	2.0
4.6	-1.3	2.5	5.1	3.7	2.6
2.7	4.1	3.0	5.3	1.5	3.2
3.3	2.9	4.6	1.8	4.0	3.3
2.1	3.8	5.4	2.3	3.1	2.7
3.7	4.3	6.9	1.8	3.9	4.6
3.4	2.6	4.1	3.9	1.8	5.5

Finish here

Analysis and synthesis

NAME_____

What did the convict say when saved from the hangman?

DIRECTIONS: Use the numbers 1-7 to solve the problems below on a separate sheet of paper. Then place the letter for each number in the decoder below to answer the riddle. **HINT:** There are no zeros in the problems and the letter "O" equals the number 2.

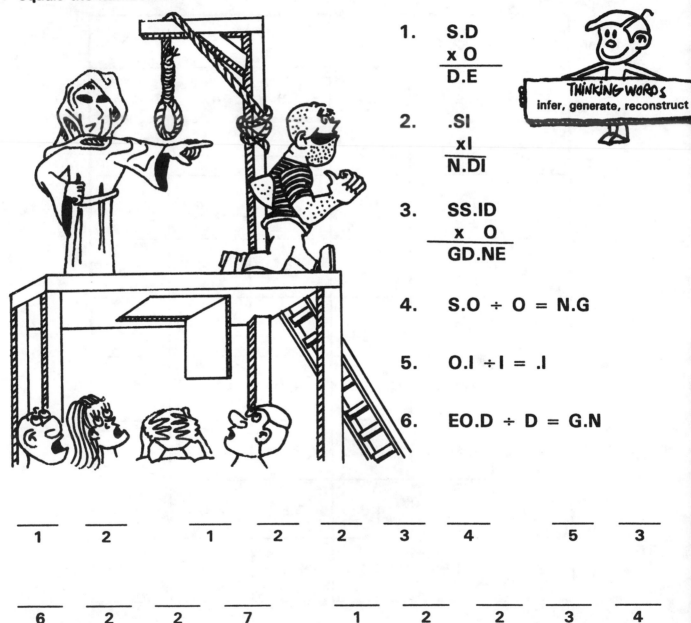

1. S.D
    x O

    D.E

2. .SI
    xI

    N.DI

3. SS.ID
    x O

    GD.NE

4. S.O ÷ O = N.G

5. O.I ÷ I = .I

6. EO.D ÷ D = G.N

THINKING WORDS
infer, generate, reconstruct

___ ___   ___ ___ ___ ___ ___   ___ ___
 1   2   1   2   2   3   4   5   3

___ ___ ___ ___   ___ ___ ___ ___ ___
 6   2   2   7   1   2   2   3   4

NAME_____

combine

integrate

relate

THINKING
WORDS

GEOMETRIC PERCENTAGES

DIRECTIONS: In this rectangular prism, first determine how many small cubes are in the whole prism. Then determine the number of each kind of small cube. By dividing the total number of cubes (in the whole prism) into the number of each kind of cube, you can find what percent of the whole each patterned shape represents.

Example:

total number of cubes   = 8
number of spotted cubes = 2

To find the percent, divide 2 ÷ 8.
The answer is .25 or 25%

Total number of small cubes _____

spotted cubes _____

white cubes _____

diagonal cubes _____

crossline cubes _____

Percent of each kind:

spotted cubes _____
white cubes _____
diagonal cubes _____
crossline cubes _____

Total number of triangles _____
spotted triangles _____

diagonal lines _____

horizontal/vertical triangles _____

plain triangles _____

Percent of each kind:
spotted triangles _____
diagonal triangles _____
horizontal/vertical triangles _____
plain triangles _____

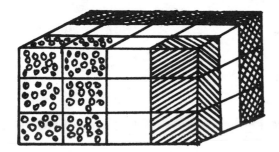

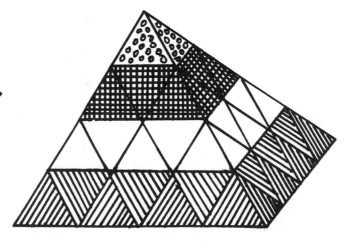

NAME_____

Going Beyond Geometric Percent

Using what you learned on the previous page, determine the percent of circles to the whole figure.

Circles = _____

Then determine the percent of rectangles and black shapes.

Rectangles = _____

Black Shapes = _____

....
: CREATE :
....

After completing the math, cut the shapes out carefully. Using 50% of the shapes, create a geometric picture. *Don't glue yet!*

Try creating a picture using 75% of the shapes. How about using 90% of the shapes?

Choose your best design and mount it on construction paper. Give your design a clever name.

NAME_____

OCTAGONAL PERCENTS

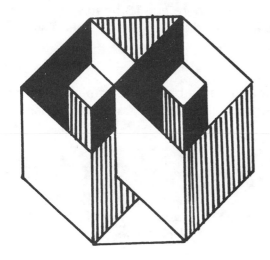

DIRECTIONS: There are 16 shapes inside this octagon. How many of the following shapes are there? (Do not count any shape with more than one color).

1. triangles _____
2. black shapes _____
3. shaded shapes_____
4. squares _____
5. white shapes _____
6. diamond shapes _____

Part Two:

To find what percent of the whole a particular shape is, divide the total number of shapes (16) into the number of the particular shape.

> *Example:* What percent of the whole are the triangles?

> 2 ÷ 16 = 12 with a remainder of 8. Since the 8 is over $\frac{1}{2}$ of the denominator, the .12 will be rounded to .13. Drop the decimal point and add the percent sign (.12 → 13%).
>
> *Triangles make up 13% of the whole octagon.*

Find what percent of the whole the other five shapes are. You will need to do you calculating on another sheet of paper.

1. black shapes _____
2. shaded shapes_____
3. squares _____
4. white shapes _____
5. diamond shapes _____

THINK WORDS

combine, integrate, relate

NAME_____

Card Deck Percentages

THINKING WORDS

combine,

breakdown,

separate, relate

combine

BACKGROUND INFORMATION: In a standard deck of playing cards, there are 52 cards. There are four different suits: hearts, clubs, diamonds, and spades. Hearts and diamonds are red; clubs and spades are black. In each suit, cards are numbered 2-10 plus a jack, queen, king, and ace. Therefore, there are 13 hearts, 13 clubs, 13 diamonds, and 13 spades in every deck of cards. This also means there are 26 red cards and 26 black cards.

DIRECTIONS: Using the deck of cards below, determine what percent of the whole deck each of the following is. An example has been done for you.

Example: 4 aces = ?
4 aces = 8%   4.0 ÷ 52 = .079 *(Round to the hundredths place. The decimal is now .08 or 8%).*

1. all black cards = _____
2. 3's and 4's = _____
3. all hearts = _____
4. all hearts, diamonds, and clubs = _____
5. all even numbered cards = _____

6. all face cards = _____
7. all red cards = _____
8. 7's, 8's, and 9's = _____
9. a two of spades = _____
10. all the clubs = _____

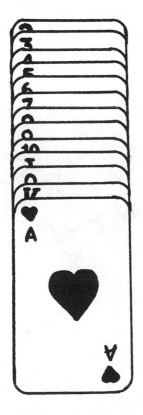

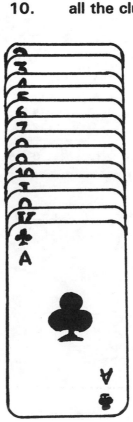

Application and analysis

NAME_____

THINKING WORDS
combine, breakdown, relate

Zorks from Nebzed

BACKGROUND INFORMATION: Zorks are inhabitants of the planet Nebzed located in the Zandromeda Galaxy. Unfortunately, there are only 525 Zorks still inhabiting this planet. No two Zorks resemble each other, and their way of life may be slightly different from yours. Find out what percent of Zorks like each of the following:

Percent of Zorks

1. Only 45 Zorks like windsurfing   _____

2. 173 Zorks engage in giraffe riding   _____

3. 406 Zorks like eating cactus jam   _____

4. 279 Zorks like bouncing on chello trees   _____

5. 342 Zorks prefer diving for Wompus fish   _____

6. 501 Zorks like picking pigwig berries   _____

7. What percent of Zorks like both giraffe riding and diving for Wompus fish?   _____

8. What percent of Zorks like both cactus jam and windsurfing?   _____

Draw a picture of how you think a Zork might look.	Write a paragraph describing your Zork.

Application and analysis

NAME_____

THE CASE OF THE MISSING PERCENTS

DIRECTIONS: Complete the percent problems below by using the numbers and percents at the bottom of the page.

1. ⬡ = 40% x 80

2. 6 = ⬡ % x 15

3. 14 = ⬡ % x 56

4. ⬡ = 30% x 6,270

5. 18 = ⬡ % x 60

6. 35 = 50% x ⬡

7. 40% x 60 = ⬡

8. 17 = 25% x ⬡

9. 52 = ⬡ % of 80

10. 16% x 90 = ⬡

11. 45% x 70 = ⬡

12. ⬡ = 37% x 80

13. ⬡ = 12% x 32

14. 21 = 35% x ⬡

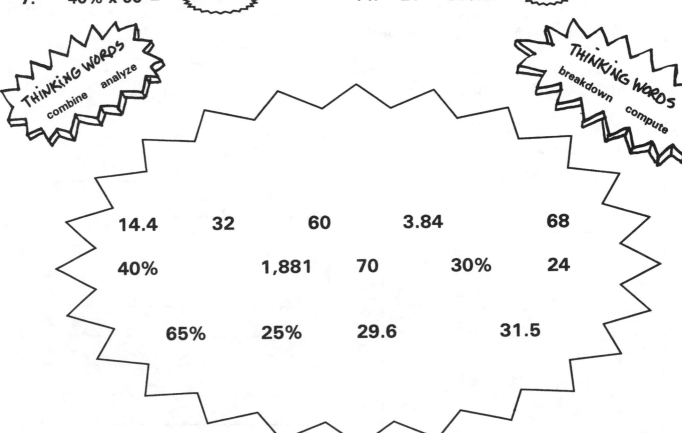

THINKING WORDS
combine   analyze

THINKING WORDS
breakdown   compute

| 14.4 | 32 | 60 | 3.84 | 68 |

| 40% | | 1,881 | 70 | 30% | 24 |

| 65% | 25% | 29.6 | | 31.5 |

ANSWER KEY

1. Answers will vary.

2. What did Dracula take for his cold? - COFFIN DROPS

3. Why did the covered wagon break down on the prairie? - IT HAD WHEEL TROUBLE

4. What did the buffalo say to his son when he went away on a long trip? - BISON

5. Hull = .165, Mast = .005, Crow's Nest = .01, Large sail = .125, Small sail = .08, Background = .615

6. Answers will vary

7. DECIMAL SKILL TEST - Decimal notation
(1) 4.3 (2) 9.026 (3) .052 (4) 7.03 (5) .296 (6) 8.0009 (7) 7.00004 (8) 643.7 (9) 3.002
(10) 8.06 (1) thirty-three hundredths (2) seven and four hundredths (3) six hundred seventy
thousandths (4) seventy-two and four ten thousandths (5) three and one tenth (6) eighty-four
hundredths (7) eight and four thousandths (8) seven thousandths (9) six hundred and forty-three
hundredths (10) seven thousand four hundred thirty-five and one hundredth

8. Cross Number Puzzle

7	3	4	9	8		
6	.	1	4	0	3	9
8	0	.	0	0	4	2
9	0	0	.	2	3	4
2	9	8	7	.	4	3
6	0	4	3	8	.	9
	3	3	7	3	0	

9. If a millionaire sits on gold, who sits on silver? — THE LONE RANGER

10.-11. Answers will vary.

12. Why are spiders good baseball players? — THEY KNOW HOW TO CATCH FLIES.

13. (1) > (2) > (3) = (4) > (5) < (6) < (7) < (8) > (9) < (10) > (11) > (12) > (13) >
(14) < (15) > (16) < (17) > (18) < (19) < (20) =

14. DECIMAL SKILL TEST - Comparing decimals
(1) > (2) = (3) < (4) < (5) < (6) > (7) < (8) > (9) < (10) < (11) = (12) < (13) >
(14) = (15) > (16) < (17) > (18) > (19) = (20) <

15. Cross-Number Puzzle No. 1

4	4	8	■	9	8	4	■
6	3	5	■	1	3	■	3
9	7	■	3	5	■	8	5
2	■	3	9	9	■	1	2
■	4	8	6	■	4	0	■
8	4	4	■	3	6	■	6
1	9	■	4	0	3	■	0
3	■	6	9	8	■	4	4

16. Tickle Your Funny Bone - PARADISE: Two white cubes with black dots
CLIMATE: What you do to a mountain

17. What did the big hand say to the little hand? DON'T GO AWAY I'LL BE BACK IN AN HOUR

18. DECIMAL SKILL TEST - Rounding (1) 612 (2) 348 (3) 87 (4) 1037 (5) 1 (6) 40 (7) 890 (8) 0
(9) 347.7 (10) .9 (11) 426.7 (12) 807.0 (13) 35.0 (14) 51.0 (15) 386.6 (16) .6 (17) 57.84
(18) 609.40 (19) .07 (20) .44 (21) 70.00 (22) .99 (23) 43.69 (24) .94 (25) .009 (26) 23.980
(27) .981 (28) .098 (29) 1.678 (30) 21.356 (31) 3.098 (32) 100.479

19. What was I? - DEINONYCHUS

20. What's Beethoven doing today? - DECOMPOSING

21. MATH BINGO- fourth column down: ($92.20; 38.36; 12.121; $4.79; 0.869

22. What do you have when 500 Indians can't buy any apples? - THE INDIAN APPLELESS 500

23. What happens if an ax falls on your car? - YOU HAVE AN AXIDENT

24. Where do mummies go on vacation? - THE PETRIFIED FOREST

25. Where does a tired artist sleep? - ON A PALLET

26. What is the title of this picture? - ESKIMO HIGH-RISE

27. DECIMAL SKILL TEST - Adding and Subtracting
     (1) 78.314 (2) 18.024 (3) 9.192 (4) 8.27 (5) $.24 (6) 9.641 (7) 9.3 (8) 3.99 (9) 8.013
     (10) 12.229 (11) 46.3 (12) 7.91 (13) 2.68 (14) $6.79 (15) 31.8 (16) 5.92 (17) 6.903
     (18) 4.779 (19) $55.66 (20) 41.322

28. Why do baby birds never smile? - WOULD YOU SMILE IF YOUR MOTHER ONLY FED YOU WORMS
29. What's the richest country in the world? - IRELAND- IT'S CAPITAL IS ALWAYS DUBLIN
30. If you had only one tooth, what would you do? - GRIN AND BEAR IT
31. TRIVIA: What am I? - (1) HONEY (2) GENERAL SHERMAN

32. DECIMAL SKILL TEST - Multiplying
     (1) 81.5 (2) 32.4 (3) 44.38 (4) 972.192 (5) $1.98 (6) .00783 (7) 1,234 (8) 670 (9) 4,600
     (10) $7.87 (11) 81.92 (12) .075 (13) 10.791 (14) 117.045 (15) 5.22576 (16) .0000024
     (17) 2.916 (18) 6.9138 (19) .72 (20) 2.7

33. How did the Eiffel Tower get its name? - FROM THE TOP YOU GET AN EYEFUL

34. Why did the tightrope walker go to the bank? - HE WANTED TO CHECK HIS BALANCE

35. What is the title of this picture? - A MENDED DONUT

36. What was Noah's profession? - ARKITECT

37. Why do dragons sleep in the morning and afternoon? - THEY LIKE TO HUNT KNIGHTS

38. Prehistoric Trivia: TRICERATOPS

39. DECIMAL SKILL TEST - Dividing
     (1) .72 (2) 1.85 (3) $14.98 (4) .66 (5) $54.45 (6) .65 (7) 13.715 (8) 78.2 (9) 34.56
     (10) $100.34 (11) 15.6 (12) .6 (13) 6.55 (14) 45.1 (15) .028 (16) 2.036 (17) .009 (18) $6.22
     (19) .832 (20) .001

40. Why was Cleopatra so negative? - SHE WAS THE QUEEN OF DENIAL

41. What is an archaeologist? - SOMEONE WHOSE CAREER IS IN RUINS

42. What do you call a cow with a newborn baby? - DECALFINATED

43. Why is milk the fastest drink? - IT IS PASTEURIZED BEFORE YOU SEE IT

44. What is another name for your funny bone? - YOUR HUMERUS

45.   Answers will vary

46.   Why did the cannibal stop eating humans? - HE GOT FED UP WITH PEOPLE

47.   Why is a rooster on a fence like a penny? - HIS HEAD IS ON ONE SIDE AND HIS TAIL ON THE OTHER

48.   What did the honeydew melon say after the watermelon proposed marriage? - YES BUT I CANTALOUPE NOW

49.   What makes doctors angry? - RUNNING OUT OF PATIENTS

50.   Animalmania: (1) SHREW (2) FLEA (3) PIRANHA

51.   How can you tell Van Winkle's trousers? - THEY'RE THE ONES WITH A RIP IN THEM.

52.   How do know that Army sergeants have a lot of headaches? THEY ALWAYS YELL TENSION

53.   What rock group kills household germs? - THE BLEACH BOYS

54.   PERCENTAGE SKILL TEST
    (1) 73% (2) 4% (3) 9% (4) 30% (5) 130% (6) .69 (7) .07 (8) .80 (9) 1.75 (10) 2.70 (11) $\frac{7}{10}$ (12) $\frac{1}{3}$
    (13) $3\frac{2}{3}$ (14) $1\frac{3}{5}$ (15) $1\frac{1}{10}$ (16) 75% (17) 16% (18) 40% (19) 210% (20) 30% (21) 8 (22) 22
    (23) 57 (24) 35.5 (25) 64

55.   What is a lunatic blackbird? - RAVEN MANIAC

56.   What do you call a cow that can't give milk? - AN UDDER FAILURE

57.   Land Area of Continents - (1) Australia (2) Antarctica (3) Africa (4) North America (5) South America
    (6) combination of Africa, Australia, and Antarctica

59-60.   Metric Castle (1) 19 cm (2) 12 cm (3) 11 cm (4) 15 cm (5) 9 cm (6) 10 cm (7) 3 cm (8) 18 cm (9) 3 cm
    (10) 23 cm (11) 9 cm (12) 6 cm

63.   Metrics Scavenger Hunt - Answers will vary

64.   Metrics - Making the right choice - (1) cm (2) cm (3) m (4) km (5) cm (6) cm (7) mm (8) km (9) mm
    (10) mm (11) km (12) mL (13) mL (14) L (15) mL (16) L (17) L (18) mL (10 mg (20) mg (21) kg
    (22) mg (23) kg (24) mg (25) g

65.   Which weighs more, a ton of feathers or a ton of lead? - THEY BOTH WEIGH THE SAME

66.   When is music like an icy pavement? - WHEN YOU WILL B FLAT IF YOU DON'T C SHARP

67.   Why does lightning shock people? - IT DOESN'T KNOW HOW TO CONDUCT ITSELF

68.   METRIC SKILL TEST - (1) m (2) cm (3) mm (4) km (5) mL (6) mL (7) mL (8) L (9) kg (10) mg (11) g
    (12) g (13) 6,000 (14) 3.89 (15) .95 (16) 49,000 (17) 7,003 (18) 48,000 (19) .358 (20) 27,000
    (21) .0293 (22) .008 (23) 920 (24) .034 (25) .78

69.   Hot or Cold? - (1) 27°C (2) -3°C (3) 100°C (4) 29°C (5) 40°C (6) 30°C (7) 0°C (8) 25°C (9) 2°C (10) 25°
    (11) 22°C (12) 26°C (13) -30°C (14) 28°C (15) 40°C

70.   It's Budget Time: Rent - 35%; Utilities - 13%; Car - 16%; School Loan - 5%; Food/Gas - 22%; Total - 91%
    Entertaintment - 9%

71.   Balanced Books: Deposits - $6,424.61; Checks - $5,356.72; Current Balance- $1,067.89

72.   Why was Adam the fastest runner? - HE WAS THE FIRST IN THE HUMAN RACE

73.   Newspaper Scavenger Hunt for Sales - Answers will vary

74.   What is the title of this picture? - PIG EMERGING FROM A FOG

76. Why did the lazy man want to work in a bakery? - HE WAS A LOAFER

77. Which way did the cowboy computer programmer go? - DATAWAY

78. Decimal Letter Code - CREATIVITY

79. A Maze of Decimals - 1→ 2.6 → .3→1.9→ -.4→ 1.2 → 2.8→ .5→ 2.1→ 3.7→5.3→ 3.0→ 4.6→ 2.3→ 3.9→ 5.5

80. What did the convict say when saved from the hangman? - NO NOOSE IS GOOD NOOSE

81. Geometric Percentages:

Total number of small cubes - 36	Percent of each kind:
spotted cubes - 6	spotted cubes - 17%
white cubes - 15	white cubes - 42%
diagonal cubes - 3	diagonal cubes - 8%
crossline cubes - 12	crossline cubes - 33%
Total number of triangles - 64	Percent of each kind:
spotted traingles - 4	spotted triangles - 6%
diagonal triangles - 28	diagonal triangles - 44%
horizontal/vertical triangles -12	horizontal/vertical triangles - 19%
plain triangles - 20	plain triangles - 31%

82. Going Beyond Geometric Percent-
Circles - 38%; Rectangles - 25%; Black Shapes- 50%

83. Octagonal Percents-
(1) 2 (2) 4 (3) 5 (4) 3 (5) 7 (6) 3   (1) 25% (2) 31% (3) 19% (4) 44% (5) 19%

84. Card Deck Percentages
(1) 50% (2) 33% (3) 25% (4) 75% (5) 39% (6) 23% (7) 50% (8) 23% (9) 2% (10) 25%

85. Zorks from Nebzed
(1) 9% (2) 33% (3) 77% (4) 53% (5) 39% (6) 95% (7) 98% (8) 86%

86. The Case of the Missing Percents
(1) 32 (2) 40% (3) 25% (4) 1,881 (5) 30% (6) 70 (7) 24 (8) 68 (9) 65% (10) 14.4 (11) 31.5
(12) 29.6 (13) 3.84 (14) 60